bliss

bliss

WRITING TO FIND YOUR TRUE SELF

★

WALKING STICK PRESS
CINCINNATI, OHIO
WWW.WRITERSDIGEST.COM

KATHERINE RAMSLAND, PH.D.

Bliss: Writing to Find Your True Self. Copyright © 2000 by Katherine Ramsland. Manufactured in the United States of America. All rights reserved. No part of this book may be reproduced in any form or by any electronic or mechanical means including information storage and retrieval systems without permission in writing from the publisher, except by a reviewer, who may quote brief passages in a review. Published by Walking Stick Press, an imprint of F&W Publications, Inc., 1507 Dana Avenue, Cincinnati, Ohio 45207. (800) 289-0963. First edition.

Visit our Web site at www.writersdigest.com for information on more resources for writers.

To receive a free weekly E-mail newsletter delivering tips and updates about writing and about Writer's Digest products, send an E-mail with "Subscribe Newsletter" in the body of the message to newsletter-request@writersdigest.com, or register directly at our Web site at www.writersdigest.com.

04   03   02   01   00   5   4   3   2   1

Library of Congress Cataloging-in-Publication Data

Ramsland, Katherine M.
  Bliss : writing to find your true self / by Katherine Ramsland.—
1st ed.
    p.   cm.
  Includes bibliographical references and index.
  ISBN 0-89879-975-9 (alk. paper)
    1. Self-actualization (Psychology) 2. Diaries—Authorship. I.
Title.

  BF637.S4 R34 2000
  158.1—dc21   00-034959
                                                           CIP

Edited by Meg Leder
Designed by Amber Traven
Cover photography from Hulton Getty/Stone
Production coordinated by Sara Dumford

For Dick Wood,
who taught me the art of reading

*

for Pelli Wheaton
who treasures authenticity

*

for Marie Gallagher,
for her enthusiasm

*

and for Jim Kerr,
without whom I might not have found my bliss.

About the Author

★

Katherine Ramsland has published fourteen books, among them biographies of Dean Koontz and Anne Rice. She has been a psychotherapist, college professor and psycho-educator, and has run workshops on Finding Your Bliss around the country.

Introduction

★

I met Diane at a conference on the spiritual nature of vocation. She was struggling over a decision that would radically change her life. She had worked in a bank for nearly twenty years, happy with the safety and security of the daily structure. However, now that her children were grown, she felt restless. Through the years, she had grown increasingly aware that she wanted to change her job and do something that felt more like a calling and not just a means to earn money—although she still needed to support herself. She wanted to feel that her work would make a contribution, as well as be satisfying to her. In other words, she wanted to be *fed* by her work.

There was one major block. She wasn't sure what she actually wanted to do, and even if she could figure it out, she wasn't sure she could make the leap from a secure job to something more entrepreneurial and uncertain. She felt paralyzed by the lack of clarity and the feeling that it would just be easier to stay right where she was. Yet something nagged at her to at least explore the possibilities.

At the time, I offered workshops in what I called Bliss Coaching, and she decided to sign up. We had to begin with the basics so Diane could formulate a sense of direction. After that, we worked on courage and commitment, and then on opportunity. Ultimately, she decided that what she wanted was to become a freelance photographer, which was not an easy switch. She had background in photography and remembered the energizing feeling that it gave her to pursue this artistic endeavor, but it had been a long time since she'd used those skills. She also needed to research the latest equipment *bliss* and take a course to bring herself up to speed. Each of these steps required that she work on her confidence and inner guidance system. It would be all too easy to just tell herself she was being foolish and walk away.

Yet once she found direction, other things seemed to fall into place. She acquired customers, first through friends and then through word-of-mouth and advertising, and she used the apparent synchronicity to build motivation and momentum. For her, the initial feeling that she needed to find herself in a new vocation paid off in a satisfying new direction. She learned what it meant to follow her bliss, and she's doing very well with it.

★ The Concept ★

It was during the late 1980s that folklorist Joseph Campbell urged people to find and follow their bliss. He had done it in his own life, to great advantage, and he believed that anyone could and everyone should. A lot of people agreed.

Briefly, by "bliss" he meant that each person has skills and talents that serve as homing devices for moving us toward what we are meant to do in life. Bliss is the natural direction we should take, the perfect work for us because it inspires maximum creativity and performance. For example, some people know the first time they put pen to page that they were born to write. It just seems inevitable. "Working with words," said a poet, "is the only thing into which I can fall and feel totally cushioned." Others feel at home with law or plants or raising children.

To discover your bliss means to wake up. Not everyone wants to do that. Sweet dreams can seem more pleasant than waking reality. It may take those sweet dreams to get started, but no fantasy can compare to the reality of finding and following your bliss. That's why it's called bliss. While our primary understanding of bliss is as a life process, it also encompasses feelings such as joy and contentment.

Keep in mind throughout this book that bliss is a metaphysical experience that begins inside. The feeling is that of a larger being calling to one of its parts to expand into it, to become whole and fully harmonious. It generates energy and optimism, and it does not necessarily arise from exclusively positive experiences. There are those who find their bliss by first entering a dark period. Whatever is within us is the material with which we have to work.

Bliss is for those of you who are interested in discovering what you are meant to do. This book came about after speaking at numerous events, including writers conferences, when I realized that many people are under the impression that creating a life direction is simply a matter of knowing what you want to do. Well, that's no simple matter and neither is acting on an inspiring idea. As I developed my teaching on the subject from seminars to workshops to a series of sessions, I realized that many people either have not recognized the correct progression or cannot stay the course. Finding your bliss means being clear, becoming motivated, staying committed and listening to your inner sense of direction.

Before going any further, it's important that you understand right away that this is a workbook. You will need to approach it with the idea that you are going to think about and do the exercises. In that case, you will need a pen and a notebook in which to keep your writings. You might as well get those items now because in a moment I'm going to ask you to do an introductory exercise.

Any of the exercises in this book can be done individually or in a group, but often a group experience can be more productive. For one thing, you're accountable to others, and for another, someone else might say something that will spark new thoughts and ideas for you. It's also fun to share personal ideas and to see how bliss begins to operate as you master the various steps. You might consider forming a bliss support group.

bliss

However you choose to approach them, keep in mind that the writing exercises are key to helping you find your bliss. A study was done that demonstrates how beneficial the act of writing is to your health—not just mentally, but physically. As reported in a recent *Journal of the American Medical Association*, 47 percent of the people with arthritis and asthma who wrote for twenty minutes on three consecutive days about something they were struggling with, showed a marked improvement in their ailments. They wrote freely, without analysis or grammatical concerns. When you write about something that matters to you, there are changes in your emotions, blood pressure and heartbeat that apparently improve your circulation. So writing is good for you. If you skip the exercises and just try to think through them, you'll miss these benefits and neglect to improve your written communication skills. In addition, you'll want a written record of your journey. Think of it as your Bliss Diary.

Having said that, let's get started with your notebooks. This first exercise is quite important to get your ideas flowing on the subject. You'll also want to refer back to it along the way to check your progress.

Exercise

Finish this thought: "Finding my bliss means. . . ."

Write as much as you want, but write at least a paragraph that includes what you think this concept means and how it applies to you personally. You will add to this as we go along, so don't worry about getting down everything you can possibly think of. Even if it's vague, just provide yourself with a written statement of how you plan to approach the work involved in this book. This is your initial statement. Give it some thought because it will form the basis of what direction you will take. Your ideas may go through changes along the way, but this first piece ought to reflect some effort in coming up with what bliss really means to you.

★ The Layout of the Book ★

Bliss presents the stages of psychological development involved in finding bliss and offers tools for getting through each stage. First, I will clarify what the concept of bliss means, and in successive chapters, I will point out the many factors that can complicate the process. Perhaps the most difficult is the exploration of your shadow side. I will then offer strategies for discovering those traits and skills that facilitate bliss and indicate how writing can be used to enhance this. Each significant step includes written exercises so you can create a personal map along the way. Sometimes you will write *before* you learn about a concept in order to get your thoughts down initially and perhaps add to them afterward. At other times, you will write your thoughts or describe your experiences at the end of a lesson. All of the exercises work together to give you clarity and motivation, as well as to help you gradually process the steps involved in finding your life direction. Writing makes your thoughts concrete. Even when you are not specifically writing, such as during a visualization exercise, you will always be asked to write something about your experience during an exercise. The point is to *use* writing to find your bliss.

Writing is an instrument, a tool that gets you to some

goal: expression, clarification, vision and creation. This book is about using writing to explore where you want to go and who you want to be. My mission is to show you how writing can help you know just what feels most "right" to you, what will make you cry out, "This is it!"

Whatever the "it" is for you, it helps to discover if it will be something stable throughout your life, such as an endeavor like poetry that you have worked at since childhood, or if it may shift as you evolve. You may find out that what you thought you wanted is not as desirable to you as something else is. In any case, writing that keeps you in touch with your feelings and thoughts can keep you focused. You will not be able to forget what you thought about because you will have it right there on paper.

I'll give you an example from my own life. It's somewhat involved, but it shows many of the steps that accompany the process. After describing what happened, I'll briefly show you how those steps apply.

When I was in high school, I was urged to go to college because it was the thing to do. If I didn't go on, I was warned, I'd never go back and I'd be stuck with too little education to do much of anything with my life. Yet I saw my friends signing up for college without having a clue what they wanted to do. The sentiment seemed to be, *Hey, what else am I going to do?*

I wasn't keen on mindlessly living my life, so instead of following suit, I hitchhiked across the country to "find" myself. After three years of doing odd jobs like acting in summer stock theater and working as a counselor in a shelter home for delinquents, I visited some friends in Arizona and looked through their college catalog.

Some of the courses looked interesting, so I signed up. I ended up loving school so much that I kept signing up every semester and summer until I ended up with some forty credits more than I needed to graduate—all because of an intense joy I had experienced from learning. I was sorry to leave, so I went on to graduate school, getting two master's degrees and a Ph.D. During that time, I became a philosophy professor.

And in high school, I had resisted ever going to college!

At any rate, since I loved the experience of learning, I thought I would really love being a teacher. While in school, I'd hung onto every word in the classrooms. My professors had opened up new worlds to me and inspired me to see how wonderfully creative the profession of teaching could be. I learned to read and write, and even to watch movies in ways I never would have if I hadn't had these enthusiastic mentors. Now I had the chance to pass along that magic to fresh young minds that I *knew* were as eager as I was for all this knowledge.

But I was wrong. Teaching was *not* my bliss. My excitement was more about the context of enjoyment in self-growth than about ultimate life direction. It was something I had enjoyed, but I soon learned it was not my calling. I felt stressed when preparing lesson plans. I came into overpacked classes full of people who were just like my high school friends had been: mindlessly becoming college students because *Hey, what else am I going to do?* This was not at all of interest to me. I wanted to work with minds as hungry as mine had been, but there were few like me and they were often overrun by the grinding gears of university demands. It seemed that I could not generate in others what I had felt in the classroom.

At the end of each semester, I was often depressed. After a few years, I was demoralized, and eventually I burned out. Was it me or them? I didn't know. I only knew that I wasn't offering anything to anyone—especially myself. I was being drained and was not the least bit happy.

So I quit and did other things. I wrote a few books, opened up a psychotherapy practice and dabbled in short-term ventures. As long as I had a project, I didn't think that much about whether I was deeply, spiritually satisfied. But sometimes it would get to me. Sometimes I felt lost. It seemed absurd that I was teaching workshops and counseling others on finding their bliss while neglecting that path for myself. I definitely could feel something lacking in my life, but I couldn't pinpoint what it was.

So I made a date with myself to go out to the desert. Literally. I spent several days in the barren but breathtaking landscapes of central Arizona, reading philosophy and writing a journal to help clear my mind and get a better understanding of what I really wanted to do. I did many of the exercises in this book to remind myself of my values and to see how I had cluttered my life with distractions. What seemed important was that I develop a mindful approach, a proactive initiative, rather than just allow things to come into my life in a random manner. I needed to know what I really wanted and that required getting grounded.

What became very clear to me were the following insights:

1. I love writing, but mostly for my own satisfaction. It gives me the feeling of being enclosed in a self-centered world, and since I don't want my whole existence to feel that way, I need to make a change.

2. I know I can teach and that students respond, but I do not like teaching at a university, and I do not like teaching the subjects I have been asked to teach.

3. I don't trust corporate values and the way people seem to lose themselves to a corporate vision, so I would not be happy teaching in a corporate environment.

4. I want to find a way to give to others, but have little time for volunteer work. If I could help educate others in a way that enhances their lives, I would like to do that kind of work, especially if it involves writing. I want to be some sort of mentor in the educational process without necessarily having to submit to the expectations of a university administration.

I didn't know quite where this left me, except that I was clear about my values: Parts of our lives should be devoted to bettering the lives of others, and I valued education, which had made my own life better. Yet I did not want to go back to being a college professor, just a small part of some educational machine that offered little to nurture the soul as an essential part of the process.

I didn't know if my retreat to the desert would make a difference in my life, but within one month of my return, I received a phone call. I was being considered for a rare and unique opportunity to direct a program that brought the humanities to the inner city, a program which included the chance for potential students to earn college credits. Known as the Bard Clemente Course in the Humanities, it had been started in New York City two years before by a man who felt as I did about education. People who could not afford to go to school were offered a free course that exposed them to such subjects as art, literature, poetry, philosophy and American history. I was offered the position at a new site.

It was as if the writing I had done in the desert had been a letter to the universe, or God, or my Larger Self, to make it known what I wanted to do and what I could do to achieve that. Once the letter was received, it was like a cosmic computer program had checked a set of fingerprints against a data bank and come up with a match.

I accepted the job, with all of its challenges, and at once felt that I had finally found a way to teach people who had the same hunger I once had and who understood that knowledge was not just an accessory, but a lifeline. Knowledge could make a major difference in the way they see the world, raise their children and create opportunities for themselves. More importantly it could stretch them and give them a way to reflect on what they *hoped* to do, not just what they *had* to do to survive. I felt satisfied and challenged all the way through my stint as director. The students understood that education could open up their lives in ways they had never imagined, and they discovered a sense of purpose and self-esteem as they achieved something important.

So that's an example of how opportunity coincides with the hard work that it takes to know what you want and to prepare yourself for it. That's the idea behind bliss, but finding your bliss involves work. You may have to do some tough self-examination. It may also involve putting together a support system. It most definitely means getting to know yourself better—both the good and the bad—and will probably mean making difficult changes. But in the end, it means coming into a track that has been there all along for you and feeling as if you have finally found the way to make the most of your potential.

The following chapters must be worked through in order for you to get the most out of this manual. You will be asked to write about experiences, make lists, speculate about situations, visualize and resolve problems. When you're finished, you will have laid some excellent groundwork for making decisions about what you want your life to accomplish.

Part One

The Basics

★

one

A Bliss Primer

★

When Joseph Campbell appeared on Bill Moyers's television documentary, "The Power of Myth," he described the spiritual interconnectedness of the world's cultures and urged viewers to "follow your bliss." As I've mentioned, he meant that each of us has a path that is uniquely our own and the most satisfying thing we can do is to follow it. "If you follow your bliss," Campbell assured us, "you put yourself on a kind of track that has been there the whole while, waiting for you, and the life that you ought to be living is the one you *are* living."

His brief counsel caught on. People everywhere tried to discover just what their bliss was and how to follow it. The slogan appeared on coffee mugs, T-shirts, book covers and bumper stickers, as if merely keeping the phrase at hand ensured that the universe would favor the owners. The idea also became a founding and guiding factor for many support groups because it offered a seemingly innovative pathway toward self-discovery and guaranteed success. People felt that if they knew their bliss, they would be happy, satisfied, spiritual and free of economic concerns. They would make it! Their potential would be actualized and unique gifts would be affirmed.

For many people, seeking bliss was a serious pursuit and some had to reevaluate their lives altogether. To really "get there" could mean leaving a career midstream, possibly taking a pay cut, and losing security or benefits, but it could also mean achieving a deep sense of satisfaction and purpose that was not evident before. Any loss was worth the gain, and there were plenty of people to testify to that.

So how do we find our bliss? And after finding it, how do we follow it? Does it happen automatically because it's part of our nature, or is it possible that we could live our entire lives and never know what our bliss was? Can anyone find it, and are there clear signposts along the way that affirm our direction? Can we make a mistake?

The truth is, finding our bliss is not automatic, in part because our culture discourages us from paying attention to our inner voices. If we can't pay attention to how we feel and what our intuitions are, we cannot develop the inner sense of direction that is essential to bliss. Our culture also encourages conformity and material gain. These influences can hinder some of us from discovering what we do best. We may confuse "bliss" with getting rich or having it all, but the idea of bliss is not a guarantee of wealth or even support. It is true that doors will open, but that's about gaining the opportunity to express ourselves more fully, not necessarily about a job offer. It is important to note that bliss is *inner*-directed, not driven by external influences even when those influences appear to offer support.

Here's an example of how we might get on the wrong track. We often confuse something we do well with finding our bliss, but that is not always the case. Anne Lamott, author of *Bird by Bird* and *Traveling Mercies*, describes how she became involved in competitive tennis while growing up and did very well. However, she also suffered from serious migraines. Eventually, her game began to slip and she realized she didn't really want to play tennis anymore, though she resisted giving up something that she was clearly talented at. She had worked very hard at it, and tennis seemed to be her best bet for a vocation. Yet ultimately she made the decision to stop. It was not what she wanted to do, no matter how good she was. Then she began to physically feel much better, and her migraines ended.

Clearly, tennis was not her bliss. Her story shows how important it is to pay attention to those signals, like persistent headaches, that tell us we are not moving along the path of joy and satisfaction. Those signals will mostly come from inside because the pressure from others is always to stick to the course and pursue what we do well. We cannot expect them to tell us differently. That does not mean, however, that we are doing what we are *meant* to do. While skills are a factor in bliss, it is not the case that all of our skills contribute to it.

Despite these warnings, it cannot be denied that for some people, doing something well may lead to their bliss and their bliss may be financially viable. For some people, it has even been spectacular.

Joseph Campbell is a good example. He spent years studying the world's cultures, looking at patterns and devising ways to understand the universal human psyche through what he found. For years, his work was known only to students and colleagues, but his passion and insight eventually grabbed the attention of people who could bring his ideas to the masses, and a new folk hero was born. Campbell's energy and obvious love of his subject inspired millions—and earned him plenty in royalties and prestige. It's doubtful that he ever imagined where his curiosity and exploration would take him. He simply followed his bliss and it paid off.

Through writing, we can concentrate on self-discovery

(our fears, our sources of confidence, our vision) and on the kinds of skills and insights we need to make bliss a practical pursuit. Although the idea that there is a life plan suited to each of us is somewhat metaphysical, there are clear steps we can take toward discovering what feels most natural and satisfying to us.

★ ARISTOTLE FOR EVERYONE ★

Despite its popular appeal, few people realize that "following your bliss" is not new. It is just a new way of phrasing an idea that goes back thousands of years. Since Campbell offered no instruction for how to figure out what our bliss is (something we need to do before we can follow it), looking at how this notion has been defined can help us develop our awareness.

The ancient philosopher Aristotle first developed the idea that we have a certain inner purpose that will unfold in what we do. He called it *entelechy*, a Greek word that means "having its end within itself." This means that we have something within us that drives us forward, coordinating our inner experiences with our external situations to develop our unique function. Positive feelings plus continuous opportunities equals progress toward bliss.

It's like this: Given all the right conditions, an acorn is going to grow into an oak tree. It's not going to be a maple tree or zebra. Its function, purpose or ultimate entelechy is to be an oak tree. It has an internal order that evolves according to a design. The acorn is in the process of becoming an oak and will reach its purpose only when it is an oak. The potential to be an oak is present in the acorn.

When applied to us, if you're born male, you'll become a man (unless you take steps to alter that through surgery). Applied spiritually, the concept gets more complicated.

It's about progress toward a goal that fulfills us. "Nature, like mind," Aristotle said, "always acts for a purpose, and this purpose is its end." We move toward balance and fulfillment.

For example, someone whose bliss urges artistic expression may respond strongly to color and texture. One man who stumbled across poetry as a boy and developed his talent said, "I was enveloped by it. It seemed the most complex, rich, full-of-possibilities sound I'd ever heard. It put images right into my brain, and I wanted to do that, too."

A mathematician expressed it this way: "It just felt right. Numbers came easily to me and it seemed right to see the universe in terms of the regularity of math. I'm not sure I *could* do something else."

An award-winning actor said, "I've always known this is what I wanted to be, as if I was born with it in my soul."

A newspaper editor told me how he moved from one opportunity to another, each of which taught him more about his skills and made him feel that he was constantly growing.

Becoming aware of our inner selves is the goal, and the inner self is the agent for achieving that goal. The idea is that, as we work on ourselves, we become who we are and who we're meant to be. We are our own "prime mover." We provide the impetus and energy to get us to our own true selves, which then becomes the ultimate expression of what makes us individuals.

The reward is this: We feel in harmony with our life process. We know why we were born. We know where we want to go and have momentum into a future. Happiness is a matter of functioning in full accord with our own true nature. And while entelechy or bliss connects us to our true nature, it plugs us into a similar evolution in our culture. If it's true that we each have an inner imperative that we can realize to our satisfaction, then it seems reasonable to assume that our species has a similar sort of drive toward actualizing its potential. Simultaneously, we can take care of our souls, as individuals and as members of a larger order.

Entelechy moves us toward our potential, but achieving it is not inevitable. It is not synonymous with fate, in the way that the mythological Greek king Oedipus had no choice but to fulfill a prophecy that foretold how he would kill his father and marry his mother. Try as he might to avoid it, his every effort moved him right into it. That's the meaning of fate. However, with bliss, we have choices. The possibilities are ever before us, but lack of faith in ourselves or adverse circumstance sometimes hamper our ability to take advantage of it. An acorn will become an oak tree only if the right amount of sun, water, nutritional soil and space are available for it to do so. Our bliss needs careful tending, and it's an ongoing process we must pay attention to at each step.

AN EXAMPLE

The actor Ving Rhames, who has appeared in *Entrapment*, *Pulp Fiction*, *Con Air* and other films, tells the story of how he defied the odds that would have put him in the streets among drug dealers and found his way to acting. It wasn't something he had thought about, but he clearly feels that he was *led* in this direction and then *called* to it. His dream had been to play football in the NFL, a common dream for many boys. However, he soon found out that his bliss would mean something else altogether.

He grew up in Harlem, surrounded by violence, crime and drugs. By the time he was eleven, he sensed that there was something in him that was greater than his situation suggested; he called it "divine intervention." He felt that he couldn't waste his life as he saw others around him doing. His mother counted on him and sacrificed a lot for him and he needed to do something with himself.

One day, he and a friend were following a couple of girls, trying to talk to them, and the girls went into a poetry class at a youth center. The boys went right in and everything changed for Rhames.

"That's where I learned about Paul Laurence Dunbar, James Baldwin, Langston Hughes and all the great black poets." He began to attend readings for the Dance Theater of Harlem, and one of his teachers told him he was gifted. Feeling confident, he auditioned for the High School of the Performing Arts and was accepted. It became one of the most positive experiences of his life, and introduced him to a world he hadn't known existed.

When he performed a scene from *A Raisin in the Sun* during his junior year, he knew that he himself had not chosen acting. The feeling that he was in the right place, doing the right thing, was so powerful and profound that he believed that God had chosen him for acting. He continued to get scholarships, which only confirmed his sense of direction. By the time he was big enough to think about being a professional football player, he no longer cared. He knew what he wanted to be, was *meant* to be.

"I look at my life," he says, "and I know that some presence or power has had a hand in it. If you just allow that hand to guide you, you'll be fine."

That's how entelechy, or bliss, works—or *can* work if we yield to it. Sometimes, however, we're not so well attuned.

★ Obstacles to Bliss ★

We humans are a complex species with the capacity to close off parts of our experiences as we move through life. For example, a woman who denies her "masculine" qualities of independence and strength may shy away from personal achievements. The same is true of a male who denies his capacity to nurture or be vulnerable.

We can resist our bliss, ignore it, buffer ourselves from it with addictions or interpret it through dysfunctional perspectives. Fear may hinder us from setting forth into uncharted territories. The urge to remain with the familiar can overwhelm the call to develop new talents. For example, someone who has just lost a teaching position may be so devastated that he fails to see the opportunity provided to discover a hidden talent. In the film, *You've Got Mail*, a woman who owns a children's bookstore goes out of business when a competitor moves into the area. She thinks her life is over, but then discovers that she knows so much about what children like that she could become a successful children's author. One loss brings out a real gain, one that she might never have realized otherwise.

Self-realization is achieved through self-knowledge— facing the truth about ourselves. For that, we have to discover those parts of ourselves that we have repressed, for whatever reason. We need to know what we're capable of before we can develop ourselves, and only by developing ourselves will we be prepared for blissful opportunities when they arise. It all works together.

Quite often, our inner guidance system will provide us with the opportunity to wake up because we are seeking balance. We may find ourselves exposed to uncomfortable situations or people who are there to bring something out of us that would otherwise lie dormant. A friend of mine, who has a neurotic need to take care of people, keeps encountering individuals who resist being mothered. Each time she feels "rejected," she is forced to examine why her good intentions are rebuffed. She has had to think about what motivates her and how she can channel her nurturing instincts in appropriate ways and deal with people on their own terms.

Growing aware of inner imbalance and then integrating the undeveloped potential can release energy to move forward. The problem is that we often have difficulty believing that, even when it's obvious. Studies have shown that people tend to put more weight on what they have invested in a past endeavor, even if it has not paid off, than in the opportunities that may lie ahead. They indulge in the notion that investment justifies further cost and they limit themselves.

I knew a man who had a dead-end job and felt depressed each and every day. He could not quit, he said, because he had to pay the mortgage. He could not try to get another job because he had no car and his current job was within walking distance. He believed that the house was all he had, but he sat in it day after day, unable to go anywhere except to work, hating his existence and seeing no way out. When someone suggested he sell the house and use the money to get an apartment and a car, which would allow him to get a better job, he refused to consider it. He had an investment in the house, and he was not going to budge. So his one asset was his trap. He had a way out, but he refused to accept it. He doomed himself to this daily boredom. Bliss was apparently not in this man's future—not if he could help it!

Bliss involves giving future possibility more allure than past investments. It means that your investment is placed where it feels liberating, not where it becomes a load. If you find yourself in a channel that has been there all along just waiting for you, it stands to reason that you'll want to get moving.

Exercise

Recall a time when you felt you were at a dead end in your life. Describe it and then recall what it was like to get back on track. If you have trouble with the image of getting back on track, envision

what might have happened if you had found an activity that provided a sense of direction. Pay close attention to the emotional
shifts as you write about this.

Then write about how important it is to recognize a dead end.

Part of the process of bliss involves knowing when to move
on, and you can learn that by making changes for the better.

★ TAKING AN UNKNOWN PATH ★

In the story by Antoine de Saint-Exupery, *The Little Prince*,
a pilot is stranded in the desert with a defunct plane. He
meets a little man who claims to be the prince of a different
planet and has recently journeyed to Earth. The prince
relates to the pilot many odd and startling observations
from his journey, especially about the habits of earthlings.
Yet as time passes, the pilot grows increasingly afraid that
he will run out of food and water before he can fix the
plane. The prince then urges the pilot to accompany him
into the desert in search of a well. The pilot does not
believe such a well exists, and even if it does, they might
never find it. Better to remain with the plane. But the
prince insists, having great faith that the well is there and
that taking the risk is their only salvation. Finally, begrudg-
ingly, the pilot agrees to leave the plane. They trudge across
the desert for some time, and the pilot's doubts turn into
serious concerns. They should never have left the plane!
He believes he could have fixed it by now, but it's too late
to turn back. Just when he feels sure they have made a
fatal miscalculation, the prince discovers the well and all
is saved.

This story illustrates the potential rewards of setting
out on an unknown path, armed only with faith in one's
abilities, which is much like discovering one's bliss.

We crave knowledge about the right direction for ourselves. We seek to have a sense of progress and clear orien-

tation. Yet clarity will not just happen. There are too many ways in which we can lose touch with ourselves, and it often begins in childhood before we even realize it's happening. Thus, before we can engage in the process of enlightenment, we need to understand how our lights have been dimmed.

Aristotle claimed that entelechy moves both internal and external forces to assist us in growing toward our goals, which is what Joseph Campbell meant when he indicated that doors would open once you made a commitment to follow your bliss. We can see the momentum of our journey toward bliss in our emotions, intuitions and circumstances.

Although I will go into this idea in more depth later, the following are feelings consistently described by people who believe they are in their bliss. They feel:

* a sense of meaning and coherence
* a sense of conviction
* a sense of direction
* fully alive
* joyful
* energetic
* creative
* powerful
* healthy
* experiences of synchronicity
* able to bounce back from stress
* they are adding to the world, not subtracting from it
* unified with their activities

Exercise

Go back to your first written exercise and list the kinds of emotions you might expect to feel if you actually pursued this direction. Check that against the list above and then write about the points of convergence and divergence. If you fall short in feeling what is described directly above, then rethink what you want to say in response to the first exercise. If you need to, write something new that will better reflect what bliss is about.

I'll remind you about these signals as we go along because they're important. If you continually feel stressed, exhausted, ill, depressed or out of synch with what you are doing, it's unlikely that you have found your bliss. In bliss, even setbacks—which are inevitable in any occupation—are taken in stride as blips in an otherwise positive enterprise. Outside bliss, stress makes negatives loom larger and feel overwhelming.

A friend of mine who had worked her way into the upper ranks of corporate management believed that because she had risen to this level of success, this must be her bliss! She interpreted the short-term victory rush after promotion as the energy and joy of self-actualization. However, once the newness of her situation wore off, she began to feel tired and depressed, and she gained weight. Eventually, she wound up with high blood pressure. This is not what happens when we find our bliss. We have to be careful about how we interpret our feelings. Short-term, situation-bound emotions rarely yield much in the way of life's direction.

Remember: Entelechy should enhance our experience of the world because it puts us in harmony with the larger picture. It gives us the feeling that we have our purpose and we're fulfilling it. We should feel peaceful and nurturing, not ready to cave in. There should be fluidity in our efforts, a sense of moving forward and being connected. We should feel actively and enthusiastically engaged in our self-guided process, knowing we are a part of something greater than ourselves.

While some people think of bliss as the feeling of euphoria, the feeling arises as the result of finding out what we're meant to do and doing it as something we love. Bliss is a process, not merely a feeling. When we experience a sense of direction and "rightness" about ourselves, we feel good. We envision a positive future toward which we are eager to move. Transitions are embraced without resistance and we can better appreciate the full range of human experience. We develop the mental flexibility to interpret as challenges what others may label as setbacks, and our lives are satisfying.

Whatever we want to call it—entelechy, self-actualization, finding your bliss—we must take the risk of going into the desert to find the well. Bliss requires self-reliance and inner resilience, as well as attention to what truly makes us happy.

Then, when we find that "track that has been there the whole while, waiting" for us, we should flow with it rather than try to control it. Like Obi-Wan said to Luke Skywalker, "Trust in the force." It's very much like that. Just let go and have faith that, once we're on the track, things will happen to help us along. We need to believe that our true purpose is in our best interest.

two

The Guidance of Care

★

It's now time to use philosophy in a more personal way. The next exercise is more involved than those you've done thus far, but it will get you thinking in a way that may be new to you. In finding your bliss, it's important to constantly evaluate your life situations along with your emotional states and tendency to remain with the familiar rather than to move in new directions. You will benefit from the ability to see yourself in the situations of others, both in terms of avoiding unproductive directions and finding positive role models. This exercise should help with both.

Exercise

Read through the following allegory, described by the philosopher Plato.

Imagine the condition of men living in an underground chamber with an entrance to the outside that involves a long passage. They've been there since childhood, chained to the floor by the leg and by the neck, so that they cannot move and can see only what's in front of them. At some distance higher up is the light of a fire burning behind them, and between the prisoners and the fire is a track with a parapet built along it, like the screen at a puppet show.

Behind this parapet, imagine persons carrying various objects, including figures of men and animals, which project above the parapet. Some of these persons will be talking. Prisoners so confined would see only the shadows thrown by the firelight on the wall of the cave facing them. And suppose that their prison had an echo from the wall facing them: When one of the people crossing behind them spoke, they could only suppose that the sound came from the shadow passing before their eyes. In every way, then, such prisoners would recognize as reality nothing but the shadows of those artificial objects.

Now suppose one of them is set free and suddenly forced to stand up, turn his head and walk toward the light. These movements would be painful, and he would be too dazzled to make out the objects whose shadows he was used to seeing. Suppose further that he was shown the objects being carried. And if he were forced to look at the firelight itself, his eyes would ache, and he might try to turn back to the shadows he could see distinctly, convinced that they were clearer than the objects.

And suppose someone were to drag him forcibly up the slope and not let him go until he had hauled him into the sunlight. Would he not suffer pain at such treatment? He would find his eyes so full of radiance that he could not see a single thing that he was now told was real.

He would need to grow accustomed before he could see things in that upper world. At first, it would be easiest to make out shadows, and then images of things reflected in water, and later the things themselves. After that it would be easier to watch the heavenly bodies and the sky by night, looking at the light of the moon and the stars rather than the sun in the daytime. Last of all, he would be able to look at the sun and contemplate its nature.

Then, if he called to mind his fellow prisoners and what passed for wisdom in his former existence, he would surely think himself happy in the chance and sorry for them. He might even decide to go back and help them become enlightened. It's likely, however, that his compassionate deed would be met with ridicule; they would tell him his sight was now ruined by going outside the cave, and "if they could lay hands on the man who was trying to set them free and lead them up, they would kill him."

Now write a brief essay in your notebook about how this allegory matches some situation in your own life, past or present.

If you're doing this in a group, have each person read what they wrote so the group can discuss it. Almost anyone can find an application of this universal story.

Once you have come up with a clear association that makes the story relevant to you, write a paragraph or so on how you think it affects your life choices. Then read how it applies to the person in the story below.

★ Bliss Coaching ★

Bliss moves us toward our potential, but achieving that potential depends on a lot of conditions being right. Finding our life direction is not inevitable, even if it's within us. One of the most difficult parts is staying committed to it, especially when the process becomes challenging in ways we had not anticipated.

Virginia was a junior high school teacher, dedicated to her job but also unhappy with it. "The hours are counter to my biological rhythms," she complained, "and the daily grind is wearing me out. I just don't feel that I have much to show for all the effort I put into it and for how tired I feel at the end of every day."

She was divorced with no children, living alone in a small town where there were few opportunities to meet people or do much of anything besides watch the junk cars rust on someone else's lawn. Virginia felt that her life was going nowhere.

She had the vague notion that she might like to be a counselor. She wasn't even sure of that, but it seemed that people came to her a lot to discuss their problems. "I think I'm a good listener," she said, "and I'd like to get trained in helping people solve some of these problems." Her plan was to go to school, more than an hour's drive from where she lived, and see how she liked it. When she talked with me about it, I suggested that she first work on clarifying her own issues and skills because that might save her some time and money. She agreed to try that.

She had had a series of dreams, and since the patterns in dreams often reveal something about what a person is struggling with, she wrote down each dream she had over the course of a week. From what she could tell, Virginia was very much afraid of something and it had to do with her family. Were she to face it, the dreams indicated, she might be overwhelmed. Nevertheless, she went to work.

Gradually, it came out that her father was an alcoholic, and she had done a lot of caretaking as a child. In the process, she had learned to develop rigid boundaries within a static set of routines for self-protection. She realized that she had probably absorbed certain patterns of behavior that supported her father's addiction, which was currently being practiced in her life by her inability to break out of her routines and try something new. She recalled that as a child, she pondered for hours the possibilities of doing things differently, yet never managed to actually put those thoughts into action. She was as paralyzed then as she was in her adult career: Virginia would think about what else she might do, but she had a difficult time following through.

She did some work with her hidden anxieties and then formulated visualization exercises for seeing herself doing those things that would move her out of her rut. As she did them, the exercises came with a lot of anxiety, so she found a way to work on visualization coupled with relaxation.

Then she began to look at her values by writing them out. She realized that as she worked on this, she felt increasingly more resistant. Finding her bliss, she believed, could mean making a serious change in her life, perhaps even moving from where she lived. The idea frightened her. She decided just to stay where she was and forget about another career. As she thought about the allegory of the cave, it occurred to her that she was going back into the dark. Nevertheless, it was too difficult for her to make the change by herself. She decided to see if a therapist could help. In other words, she sought someone who could help her leave the cave and see that the daylight was a wonderful place.

Exercise

Put yourself in Virginia's position. Imagine what fears might hinder you from moving forward. Now write about what it would be like for the next year if those fears influenced you more than your desire to be happy.

If you feel as Virginia did, think about what you might do to overcome the anxiety. If you think you can move beyond your fears on your own, write down three things you need to do to accomplish that. Make these items part of your Bliss Diary by noting how they will assist you in your life direction.

★ FOLLOWING YOUR VALUES ★

One of the most difficult steps in finding your bliss can be clarifying your values.

Generally, I ask people to think about what they would say to persuade someone who is not easily convinced to do something that they think is important to do. The following examples will demonstrate some of the various paths that people have taken to achieve this.

In one workshop full of mothers of all ages who were trying to get ahead, I urged them to write an essay about what mattered to them and to write as if they were telling it to a friend. Almost unanimously, they said they had a hard time putting that into words, so we discussed it as a group. One young woman said she wanted to help women stuck in abusive relationships "to see the kind of prison they were in and to understand that they needed to get out." She based this concern on her own experience, still incredulous that she had remained in such a place herself. I told her to address her "letter" to another woman caught up in such a relationship.

"Think about it in terms of Plato's cave allegory," I told her. "You're the one who got out, and now you feel the need to go back in and rescue others from their blindness. The guy in the allegory didn't fare so well, but maybe you can think of a way to do it that wouldn't be resisted. Think about how you would have reacted while you were in that situation, and find a way to get your message across to the person you once were."

That helped her to put into words why her life now was better than her life stuck in a bad relationship. The others, however, were still having a difficult time knowing what they cared about and what difference that could make.

To give them an example, I used the inspiring story of Ben Carson, who wrote *The Big Picture*. He grew up in Detroit without a father and with seriously limited opportunities. Despite these circumstances, his mother believed her children could succeed. She kept them off the streets, which would have been like being chained in the cave, by encouraging them to read. Unlike many young black men in his neighborhood, Carson made it through high school. He then went to Yale and got into medical school. After working very hard, he became a world-renowned surgeon and is currently the director of pediatric neurosurgery at Johns

Hopkins. He bettered himself against the odds by reminding himself that he had a purpose. While that purpose may have been difficult to achieve, the uphill battle to get out of the cave and see the sun was well worth it.

Acknowledging this story, a woman named Laura asked me how she could make an argument for showing her kids, who never read, that education was important to their future. She was taking college courses for this very reason, but she had not yet exhibited any clear benefit from them in her life. Her children resented the time she spent away from them; she was feeling guilty, but was still determined to show them the importance of the choice she was making. In other words, it was all still abstract, and she wanted a way to show them in concrete terms how education can make a difference.

"The next best thing," I said, "is to show it in someone else's life." I told her about Homer Hickam, who wrote about how he developed a dream as a boy to one day become a rocket scientist in his book *October Sky*. Since he lived in a poor West Virginia mining town, such a dream seemed absurd to those who were used to thinking of their lives in limited terms, including Homer's parents. One teacher encouraged him, but everyone else tried to get Homer to stop dreaming. He listened to his heart. Each day he walked eight miles to get to an open field so he could experiment with the rockets he had designed. Many of them were failures, but he kept trying. At one point, he gave up, and his family told him that he was now doing the right thing. However, his initial vision returned, he continued his work, and he eventually won a state and national science fair. The prize made it possible for him to go to college. In the end, he became a scientist at NASA.

Hickman's story clearly displays how our values can direct our lives. Values provide the staying power of vision. When we care about something, we keep working at it.

The women in my workshop now had a clear picture of what they could look at in their own lives. They also realized that there are many ways to follow your values, but all of them require vision and perseverance.

★ Bliss as a Calling ★

bliss
THE GUIDANCE
OF CARE

Bliss *is* a calling. Once you know what it is, you feel as if it has been set up for you by some outside force that knows and guides you. This is not about wanting something badly. It's about what one writer said of the experience of writing: "You write because you can't *not* write."

However, I can't stress enough how important it is to realize that just wanting to do something is not necessarily a sign of bliss. Wanting to do something may have more to do with a personal agenda or an impression you want to make. I had a friend named Peter for whom things always seemed to work out just right. He developed himself through several promising careers, but ultimately decided that he really wanted to be a writer, so he quit everything else to concentrate on that. He believed that since he felt strongly about it, wanted it badly and had always made a success of whatever he set out to do, that this was just going to happen for him. Doors would magically open.

Then I read one of his manuscripts, and it was clear that he did not really have the talent for writing. His grammar was poor; his sense of structure and pace nonexistent. I mentioned this to him, and he said that someone else would take care of all of that once he got a book contract. He was convinced!

When nothing happened right away, he began to write letters to the editors to whom he had sent his manuscript. I happened to read some of them and was surprised by his demanding tone. It wasn't long before his letters contained lies about nonexistent publications in an attempt to make himself look better. Clearly, he was getting desperate, and this fear was motivating him to do things he was not proud of. Yet I knew that he would not have success with this, since the manuscript was in such poor condition.

Peter was mistaking manipulation with the idea that doors would open. He was trying to force them open just because it was what he wanted. He had an agenda that had more to do with his self-esteem and how he presented himself to others (as a winner) than a genuine sense of wanting to find and follow his bliss. He had already told people that he was going to do this and he was going to succeed. Now he seemed desperate to prove himself.

This is a good example of how one's fears, desires and dreams can actually throw you *off* the track of your bliss. Rather than learning what his bliss actually was, Peter took matters into his own hands and tried to force them to work into his plan. Eventually he realized that this was not the way to succeed. He was feeling stressed and angry, and his behavior was becoming increasingly more secretive. It didn't take him much longer to recognize that bliss and tension do not coexist. Peter reexamined his ideas about what he wanted and reevaluated his actions in light of what he knew about the well-being of bliss. He let go of the idea that he was meant to be a writer, and as soon as he did, he felt immensely relieved. As he put it, "A calling should feel wonderful and fulfilling. It should free you to do your best, not enslave you to some goal."

★ Bliss as a Quest ★

In order to see how bliss can give you a sense of perspective about your life, think of finding your bliss as a quest. The universal pattern of a quest goes something like this:
* Following day-to-day routines
* Having a heightened awareness of something that

needs to be done
* Ignoring it
* Encountering a person or event that will remind you of this need
* Accepting the task and crossing the threshold
* Encountering challenges, including the need to assess support networks
* Approaching the largest hurdle

* Struggling and maturing; utilizing your supports
* Getting the reward
* Using your enlightenment for the greater good

You may find this pattern useful in your own quest for bliss.

Exercise

Look over this pattern, and then match it to something from your own life that indicates a calling to which you need to respond. Try to imagine the obstacles, as well as how you might overcome them. Then think of ways of how getting the reward will help others.

Write a paragraph about how what you just wrote is related to the first exercise on what bliss means in your life.

While the experience of bliss lays out like the universal pattern of a calling or quest, let me be more specific:

A woman I know named Danielle worked in a corporate job making a lot of money and getting a lot of affirmation for her talent in management, but she knew it was not what she wanted to do. What she actually wanted was to run off with the circus as a trapeze act, but since that seemed impractical, she ignored this desire. Then she had the chance to take lessons in trapeze just for the fun of it, so she did. It reminded her of her dream.

Danielle definitely had a talent for it and loved it so much that she yearned to find a way to make money at it. She envisioned gathering together a troupe of people to put on shows, and eventually they came her way. She "crossed the threshold."

She wrote a few shows and found an old theater with a stage that she could use. Next, she offered her hometown a few shows. She found friends who lent their support. Her show proved to be a success, and she then saw bigger things. She wondered if she ought to take her show on the road, playing in larger cities. It was one thing to play to a local group, comprised of people she knew, and quite another to get a larger audience to take her seriously. It also meant quitting her job. She went ahead and did it. Although she didn't make the same amount of money, she was exceedingly happy to be doing what she wanted on a full-time basis. She then used her talent and troupe to design entertainment that would also be a spiritual experience for those who saw it.

Danielle was beckoned toward a quest, and she succeeded at taking up the challenge. She succeeded because she became aware of needing something more. Danielle knew what her vision was, what it would mean to see it through and what kind of support she would need to help her stay committed.

Once you are aware that you need to make a change, clarify what that change will be. That comes from assessing your values, skills, interests and opportunities. As Danielle thought through her vision, it became clear what she cared about, what she could actually do about it and how she could develop it.

Then you need to learn how you block and how you facilitate your momentum, so that you can use what works to keep yourself committed and on track. Danielle knew that a secure job could hinder her, so she started into her new venture slowly, simply as a hobby. Once she saw how happy it made her and how much talent she really had, she was able to take the leap.

As your commitment gets tested—as it surely will—you must develop a support system and learn how to tap your energy for maximum power. You must also develop a clear image so you can recognize when the right people have come into your life to open doors that will put you on the right track.

As you move in the direction that will best affirm who you are, you will experience the euphoria of self-actualization, creativity, peak performance and a sense of being larger than yourself. That's the ultimate reward, as Danielle discovered, and it comes with a responsibility: You need to become a channel for the forces of bliss to help open doors for others.

★

Given all that has been said in this chapter, it's important to get to the basics of how you can create a vision: learn what you cherish. Go on to the exercises below.

Exercise

To gain some clarity about what you value, write about the following:

1. Describe the last time you felt challenged in a way that inspired you.

2. Is there anything from your past that still plays a role in your life today?

3. Has there been a person in your past who has greatly influenced you? Describe him or her and how that person influenced you.

4. Is there something in your life at present that has major importance for who you are as a person?

5. Is there a person in your life whose support you can count on? Describe an incident in which that person came through for you.

6. Is there something in your life that will have a major influence on how you will move toward your future?

7. Is there a future goal that will play some significant part in how you live right now?

To assess when you're not centered, write about the following:

1. List things that frustrated you as a child.

2. List things that frustrate you now.

3. Compare one and two, and list the similarities and differences.

4. What are your typical reactions to frustration?

5. How might those reactions hinder you in reaching a goal?

6. Describe the last time you were bored or depressed.

7. Describe what it was like to set up a goal and to fail to follow through.

Look over what you have written for both parts of this exercise and try to summarize who you are when you are centered. Make a list of feelings that arise from that, including your physical sensations, quality of attention, engagement in a situation and sense of rightness.

Then make a list of feelings that arise when you feel off-center. Bookmark this section of your notebook because you will be referring to it again. You will use this list to judge when you are on or off your track because your bliss will be attuned to those things you value; when you're getting away from that, you'll be able to read your wrong direction in your other feelings.

Keep in mind that your bliss is not necessarily about how you may want to impress others, but about what you are called to do based on your unique potential.

three

The Will to Flow

★

Best-selling suspense author Dean Koontz spent the early part of his career writing just about anything to keep ahead of the bills. As he became more successful, he was able to spend more time developing plots and characters. The more he wrote, the more he knew he was born to write and the better he got at it. He also got a lot more successful. For him, finding his bliss really paid off, and he was finally able to relax. As he did so, he developed a rhythm that offered him an unexpected bonus.

One day, while writing his book, *Watchers*, he had an experience that introduced him to the heightened creativity that comes with the right balance of challenge, deep concentration and talent. The book, about a dog with artificially developed human intelligence, initially had been difficult to write; Koontz said it had taken some eight months to write the first two-thirds of it. Toward the last third, however, when he had gained a clear sense of direction coupled with the feeling of control and spontaneity, he had an incredible experience. The pages seemed to write themselves. "It just flew," he said.

He began to write fast and did not stop, save for one

break, for two days. "I got up one morning and went to work. I ate a sandwich at my desk, kept going, worked around the clock and finally fell into bed the next evening, totally exhausted. I slept that night, and the next morning got up and worked twenty-four hours straight. In the first session, which was about thirty-six hours, I wrote something like forty pages. In the second session, I wrote around forty pages in even less time. That's about thirty thousand words in two sessions, and it needed almost no revision."

He got into flow.

★ The Will to Flow ★

I'm going to describe flow, one of the most delightful aspects of finding your bliss, because I want you to have something to look forward to as you move through the process of self-discovery. Flow happens in moments of peak performance and is enhanced by doing an activity that is completely satisfying. It is the experience of complete absorption in an activity that, in retrospect, becomes perhaps the most wondrous part of that activity. But before we go any further, let's start with a bit of writing.

Exercise

Have you ever participated in an activity in which you felt larger than yourself and completely in touch with what you were doing, even to the point where you seemed to be performing much better than usual? Describe the activity and what it was like for you. Close your eyes and try to reexperience it so you can get as many details as possible. We'll return to this piece of writing later.

★ The Experience of Flow ★

Flow is the sense of absorption we get when we're concentrating so deeply on a task that we feel at one with it. Time stands still and we grow less engaged with our external environment. Music may be playing, people may be talking, machines may be clicking, motors may be running, but we remain "blissfully" unaware of them. We are fully engaged, involved in our task. We do our best work at such times and the more often we can get into that state, the more likely it is that we're moving toward, or are actually participating in, that which we will recognize as our bliss. Taking a new step, said Russian author Fyodor Dostoevsky, is what people fear most, but experiencing the state of flow may motivate you to do it anyway. Whatever your bliss is, you will experience an inner imperative, a feeling of rightness and a sense that you cannot do anything else and be as creative or as satisfied.

The other day, I watched a young woman named Suzanne as she cut and styled my hair. She was tall, thin, well-dressed in dark knits, and her own short dark hair was styled in a unique manner. She seemed quite caught up in what she was doing, so I asked her if she loved her work.

"I really do," she told me.

"What made you decide to do this line of work?"

She shrugged as if no explanation should be necessary. "I'd always sort of thought about it," she said with a smile, "but when I was in high school, everyone discouraged me from going into it, so I went to school for accounting. After a year of that, I knew that this is what I wanted to do, so I went to school and got my license, and I've been working at it for several years. I'm glad I went ahead with it."

"And what's it like to do this all day?"

She smiled. "I just get into the rhythm of it. I don't even notice the time. It never really seems like work to me. I want to do this the rest of my life."

She was in flow. Having found her bliss, she was relaxed and satisfied. Thus, she was able to allow her work to draw her fully in. It became like a trance, but one that she could recall well enough to know how much she enjoyed it.

The concept of flow has been closely linked to the Japanese practice of Zen. "If one really wishes to master an art," said D.T. Suzuki, author of *Zen and Japanese Culture*, "technical knowledge is not enough. One has to transcend technique so that the art grows out of the unconscious." A central concept of Zen is the idea of "oneness," becoming inseparable from the essence of what you are doing. It means being totally present as you connect yourself to your task. You *become* what you are doing, which then extends your perception beyond ordinary limits.

Flow is about our best functioning as individuals; we find our niche and do it so well that we feel fully satisfied and successful. The work we do feels like quality work, and we believe that our time is well spent. According to psychologist Abraham Maslow, we all need work that will be meaningful, creative and worthwhile. It's not just about survival or making money, but about fulfillment and development. These things are important for our health and prosperity. Meaningful activities motivate us to keep doing them and to keep getting better at doing them.

Psychologist and University of Chicago professor Mihaly Csikszentmihalyi, the expert on flow, made the first significant studies of this phenomenon. He wanted to find out if it was universal rather than something unique to Zen practitioners. To him, it was motivated from within and was the aspect of work that was perceived as meaningful during intense, focused concentration. A person in flow works with a sense of purpose as well as an instinct for how to achieve that purpose. It's an organic process, beginning inside, in which personal desire and behavior come together and flow into a sense of achievement; it produces a sort of pride in ownership. It's about craftsmanship—caring about what you're doing—as opposed to just working at something. Csikszentmihalyi went on to study this phenomenon with surgeons, artists and mountain climbers who had reported feelings of great joy from complete immersion in what they were doing. He then expanded his work to other areas, including creativity, and ended up writing an entire book on the subject called *Flow: The Psychology of Optimal Experience*.

"Action follows upon action," he stated, "according to an internal logic that seems to need no conscious intervention by the actor. He experiences it as a unified flowing from one moment to the next, in which he is in control of his actions, and in which there is little distinction between self and environment, between stimulus and response, or between past, present and future." While flow seems to occur spontaneously, it can be harnessed into a more regular and sustained experience. "People who learn to control their inner experience," he claims, "will be able to determine the quality of their lives."

What better indicator of bliss could there be?

When consciousness feels harmonious in the pursuit of some activity, people pursue that activity for its own sake rather than for some extrinsic reward. In other words, it feels good to them, and they don't worry about whether they will gain in some material way from it. They relax into it and become absorbed by it.

Flow gives us the energy for and the experience of becoming more centered. "I have enough energy," said a flight attendant who loved her job and had experienced flow, "that I feel I can give more of myself to others and still not be drained."

Flow can also be applied to peak performance in business and in sports, among other things. It is what athletes call "being in the groove," "playing out of one's head" or being "pumped up" or "wired." Others have called it "the white moment," the "optimum state" or "the zone." Most of them are doing what they feel is their life calling, and flow is the bonus. If bliss were a car, flow would be the fuel.

In short, flow is the context for excellence. It helps us to do our best. Generally, it feels effortless, although in truth it results in one's best work. A tennis player might reach an "impossible" ball or, like Koontz, a writer might suddenly break out of concentrated work to the feeling of gliding and just being the vessel through which the words express themselves. As Suzanne the hairdresser said, it doesn't really feel like work, although it usually produces the best work you've ever done.

Exercise

Now that you're more familiar with the idea of flow, look at what you wrote in the first exercise in this chapter and write a page or so relating it to what you wrote when you thought about what bliss means to you. Describe how you think the experience of flow could become part of the work you envision for yourself. If you have trouble, look back at the experience Dean Koontz described and use that as a guide.

★ How People Experience Flow ★

There is a difference between flow, which inevitably involves a feeling of quality, and simply doing hack work quickly. It has to do with state of mind, honed abilities, confidence and experience. At such times, creativity and energy feed off each other, minimizing external distractions to the point of perceptual blunting. You're not aware of time passing, or that you're hungry, or that the phone is ringing.

The person in flow can perform for hours, as Koontz did, without noticing anything else that might be happening. Time seems simultaneously to be faster and slower, and the person feels utterly unified with the task at hand. There's no stopping. There's just the thing itself. The person in flow is completely present, attuned to the moment.

"The dancer becomes the dance," Louis L'Amour once said, "and I am the writing."

It can happen in any profession because it has more to do with how the person feels about his or her work than about the actual work.

A music teacher put it like this: "There are times when I become absolutely absorbed in the music, 'at one' with it, if you will, and feel as if I'm an extension of the music itself." Echoing her, a researcher said, "It's almost as if the mind is being driven by some other force that's at some other level of being. It's like thinking and not thinking at the same time, and suddenly everything becomes easy."

"I'm just in my own world," a stonemason said. "Nothing else matters."

A clergyman found that ideas emerge during this state that surprise him, while a computer mechanic described the trancelike qualities: "There are times when I'm fixing a hard drive, and I lose track of time. The phone will ring and I can't be bothered. I'm totally focused on finding that one bad part." An accountant confirmed this aspect of flow in his own work: "Sometimes I become so absorbed, I'm not aware of anything around me. Everything becomes so distanced, or else I've become so within myself that I can't hear or see anything but the problem I'm working on."

Flow stretches people beyond their perceived limits. It bonds them with their work, yielding both stamina and euphoria, which continues to make their work exciting. "Flow," wrote Csikszentmihalyi, "is the way people describe their state of mind when consciousness is harmoniously ordered, and they want to pursue whatever they are doing for its own sake."

There's a paradoxical element as well. Although it may appear to be effortless, flow does evolve from discipline and skill. It's a sort of relaxed intensity. The best conditions for optimizing it come from a balance of focus, motivation, organization, vision, energy and the ability to allow inner resources to be freely expressed. "I have to be committed to it," an entrepreneur said, "and prepared for it, or I won't get the full experience."

Centering attention on what you're doing in this trance-like state distorts your perception of time and blocks the hindrances that often arise when you get too self-conscious about your work. An easy yet unwavering rhythm develops. Thought and motion become single-minded intention. The person just lets go and operates on automatic pilot. People in flow report feeling "most alive" or "at full throttle"—a sense of having been transported into a newer and sharper reality.

"If I could do this all the time," said Koontz, "I could write a book in ten days, and it would be of higher quality than what comes with endless struggle. You look at something like what happened with *Watchers* and say it's uncanny. How is it possible for me to write at the same level on those pages when I struggled with all these other pages at the rate of two or three per day? When I look at the results, it's actually better than stuff I worked on for a longer period of time. Those are the moments that seem like a form of meditation, or a connection with something else. It's phenomenal. I worked all day and right through the night and into the following afternoon—yet it was only in the last hour or two that I began to feel tired. Then I crashed totally. But there was no sense of weariness while I was writing, no sense of time passing. That is definitely an altered state of consciousness. Everything is coming at you like an avalanche and you're not able to get up and walk away. You're so into it, you don't even realize how long you've been there. You have this ebullient, joyful feeling."

Even more interesting is the way flow can maintain itself. I once had the experience of being deeply engrossed in a project when my computer suddenly quit working, and even destroyed what I'd been writing. This threw me into a sort of limbo: I was still half in flow—I was the words, the images, the characters. It was all still there, churning inside me, but I had lost the medium for expression. I got the computer back up and threw myself into a frantic attempt at reconstruction, working for about ten hours until I felt I had it right. I could not eat, could not speak coherently to anyone who came into the room, could not engage in anything else until I was finished. I did try to take a break for dinner, but my mind was so engaged in the flow of the project that I abandoned everything but the project.

Others have described to me their personal engagement with a project that enhances getting into flow. A pipe fitter stated, "It's *my* work. My name is on it. It will last and I'll feel good about it. Pride in a job well done is better than money." A secretary viewed it as her contribution to the reputation of the company and that made it meaningful to her.

Although flow cannot be forced, there is a certain amount of preparation one can do, and that will be discussed in a later chapter, after you've done some of the preparatory work yourself.

★ Stages of Flow ★

The onset of flow comes with a feeling of excitement and energy. "My heart beats fast," said an actress, "and I notice how incredibly accelerated I am in what I'm doing." Some people describe a bit of anxiety while others feel very attuned and clearheaded.

As flow sets in, the work pace increases as the rhythm picks up. There's a certain feeling of fluidity. Perception, imagination and manual operations function at a higher than normal level. "My senses are especially sharp or in tune," said a psychotherapist. "I pick up on the slightest change in a client and quickly seem to understand its purpose."

The person in flow has a body instinct for what is happening. Thought and motion seem perfectly integrated as awareness narrows. Flow may be experienced in a single time frame, or may arch over a period of time that is punctuated by nonflow events. My brother, a machinist, talked about how he was able to come back to work each day and pick up a project right where he left it, getting back into this heightened performance almost immediately. "The experience is like daydreaming," he said, "only my body has not stopped working." A utilities foreman said that he can take a phone call and then continue his work without any interruption to his concentration. Even a market researcher described how he was unable to concentrate at first amidst all the voices talking on other phones, doors slamming and pressure to meet deadlines. Soon, however, he settled into the project. "I revved into high gear without realizing what had transpired and tuned everyone else out. As I gathered momentum, the figures fell into place, the questionnaires got completed and I met my impossible deadline."

Thus, flow comes in as excitement, deepens into heightened performance and almost a trancelike state, and comes to an end as the person moves back into ordinary levels of awareness. It's like diving deep into water, experiencing oneself in a completely different world and then emerging again from the depths. A psychologist said that she feels a twinge of apprehension when she feels her concentration coming to an end. It's like someone about to enter the room and interrupt her. One idea starts to trip over another because she no longer feels the flow. At any rate, it can be over fairly quickly, leaving you with a sense of exhilaration over the work you've performed and possibly a sense of disappointment that things feel so mundane again. With reorientation comes the awareness that you're hungry, cold or need to get up and stretch. You may be completely fatigued. It's almost as if you've been utilized to channel some highly creative spirit and you need to get reenergized. You may not even believe all that you have accomplished or remember much of what you did during the time of flow. It really is an altered state of consciousness. In fact, as I wrote this chapter, I managed to complete nine pages in one sitting, and I can't quite believe I was able to sustain my attention that length of time. I seemed to have been on automatic pilot.

Those who have described the most intense and sustained periods of flow and who experience them regularly are people who believe they are doing what they are meant to do. They have found fulfilling work and have developed an easy rhythm with it that makes a deep state of flow more likely to occur. While flow is not the ultimate goal of bliss, it is one of the clearest feelings of affirmation that bliss is at hand and is a wonderful thing to experience.

Exercise

Look over the following list of traits that describe the experience of flow.

Mental calmness

Complete absorption

Lack of external stimulation

Positive energy flow

Feeling of being in control, yet challenged

Relaxed concentration

Trancelike but engaged state

Sense of ease of effort

Feeling of inspiration or creativity

Mental clarity and alertness

Intuitive responses

Sense of joy or euphoria

Now write a more detailed description than the one you did earlier about a peak experience you have had at some point in your life. Describe the set of circumstances you think facilitates complete absorption in an activity, whether it is a game, a sport, your work, cooking or some other activity.

If you are working in a group, have several people read their experiences. If not, ask one other person you know to write down how they felt when they were doing their best work in a state of flow. Compare the two descriptions and see where they share similar qualities.

Bookmark this exercise for reexamination when we revisit the concept of flow later in the book.

I will return to flow after we do more work with the initial steps of finding your bliss. I wanted to give you a taste of the wonderful things that lie ahead, but now it's time to do some personal work. The next chapter offers you a look into some of the neglected parts of yourself.

four

SHADOWBOXING

★

I believe you can find your bliss only when you gain good grounding in self-knowledge. The next two chapters work together to provide you with opportunities to discover aspects of your life that can hold you back from what you most want to do, and they are followed by a chapter that pinpoints those traits more specifically. The concept of the "shadow" offered in this chapter is complex but necessary, and the technique of double reflection presented in chapter five provides a way to better access it within yourself. Developing this kind of self-awareness for things you may not want to know can be difficult, but when you realize that the same techniques will help you see what you have going for you, you may appreciate the value of this exercise. Most people go about their lives without any such awareness, but you are trying to become one of those unique people who is deeply satisfied with your work.

Continuous self-examination is an important process in the development of inner authority, which is an essential part of finding your bliss. You need to be able to check your feelings as you set out on your path and to remain aware of new insights that surface from unique situations. We encounter many things along life's path that make us question the decisions we make. Sometimes those challenges come from within us: Self-doubt, hesitancy and second-guessing are often rooted in our own issues. A look at your shadow side may help you to better see what those issues are and how they may hinder your journey to bliss.

A few years ago, I had finished a writing project and was not sure what I would be doing next. That's very difficult for me. Usually I have something else started by the time I finish each project, but not in this case. I like to have structure in my life and some sense of what my future holds. I started looking into doing things other than writing to support myself, even though I was sure that writing was my path. When several proposals were turned down, I started to panic a little. A friend of mine who had good intuitive skills suggested that I just wait. I knew I was not in a position to trust my own intuition, since I was operating out of fear, so I listened to him.

He had a feeling that forcing myself to develop patience and perseverance in the face of my insecurities would be good for me, and that it would even yield something unexpected. I didn't doubt that, but I questioned the wisdom of not taking up opportunities for other sorts of jobs when they came along. Then two more people echoed my friend's advice, and I had to believe that there was something behind it, a message to which I should pay close attention. A psychic even told me that my next book would emerge from the one I had just done, but I couldn't see what he meant by that. I also didn't know whether I even believed him. I could not envision another book at all, let alone one that would grow out of my previous work.

In other words, I was being blocked by something and was no longer on my track. My own intuition was diminished. Yet when several messages of the same type come to me from different sources, I generally give that some weight. If they are helping to free me from fear rather than adding to it, I listen. The idea of bliss is to grow lighter, not heavier.

So I waited. And it was very difficult. There were days when I thought I was being foolish and other days when I really got scared. I picked up tennis as a way to pass the time and wondered when I would find out what this "waiting" was all about. (Obviously, I'm not good about being contemplative.) Finally, a project came my way, unannounced, from another writer. While I immersed myself in reading it, I suddenly *knew* with the full force of conviction what I would do next; in fact, it came out of the book I had just written. I quickly developed a proposal and sold the book. Looking back, I realized that had I taken up any other opportunity during that "waiting" period, I'd have been unable to write this other book because it needed to be done as soon as possible and would demand all of my time and attention. This experience taught me about my shadow side, or inner wound, and how my fears and needs can hinder me along my path.

Let's move on to the psychological mechanics of bliss in terms of personal traits that block it. I've just offered an example of how my fear of financial insecurity nearly knocked me off my track. Now I will describe what is at work in this kind of situation.

Many of us disown our inner authority sometime during childhood before we've learned to trust it. Some adult or peer tells us that our ideas are without value or are wrong, and we tend to lose faith in ourselves. This diminishes our wholeness. We start to block and repress things, and then we forget some of those things that once were part of us. However, those repressed things don't go away. They remain part of us, but we cannot see them, and they still influence how we feel and behave.

Just to reiterate, until you find bliss and live it, you

are not wholly yourself. You have a larger self calling you to become fully realized. It may seem logical to conclude that we'd all want to respond to that, but we develop blind spots and comfort zones that sometimes keep us limited and undeveloped. We need to examine those parts of ourselves that we either can't see or we avoid, so we make sure they aren't blocking our bliss.

The steps are as follows:

1. Learn about the shadow.
2. Understand how it applies to us.
3. Develop a technique to become more aware of it.
4. Use that awareness to identify our personal bliss blockers.
5. Use that awareness to identify our personal bliss facilitators.

★ The Shadow ★

According to Swiss psychiatrist Carl Jung, who developed the holistic notion of consciousness, the human psyche is comprised of several dimensions: the conscious and the unconscious. In the conscious realm, we emphasize order and rationality, but we equate the unconscious with chaos. It's something we're often afraid to examine. It contains instinctual patterns, sense perceptions and feelings that we repress—"the part of us," according to Jung, "that we don't want to be part of us."

The basic structure of the psyche is expressed in fundamental emotional patterns, called archetypes. These are universal experiences and they become real to us through images such as the innocent child, the wise old man, the great mother, the hero or the descent into hell. Archetypes show up in the arts, literature, mythology, religion, dreams and cultural rituals. They transcend time and place, and their value lies in how strongly we respond to them. A good example is the movie *Star Wars*, which, in 1977, had such widespread appeal that audiences returned to see it over and over.

The archetypes in this film were numerous and compelling: the hero's quest, the wise old man, the invisible power that guides us, the fair maiden who must be saved, the outlaw adventurer, the dark warlord with secret powers and so on. George Lucas certainly understood those archetypes that were most potent for us, and people in many other countries were caught up in it as well.

The shadow is one such archetype, and it takes several forms. Its abstract manifestation—Darkness—is viewed as absolute evil that stands against absolute good. This is a universal pattern of consciousness. Every culture has a sense of good and evil. There is also a personal shadow, which forms from the way we're raised. We learn from our families and the culture at large what it means to be "good"—the behaviors to emulate—and what it means to be "bad"—the behaviors to shun. When we conform to these standards, we try not to feel, think or act in ways that contradict the self-image we seek. In other words, if "being good" means never to tell a lie, we will try not to lie. If we end up lying, we will keep that a secret to ensure that others still see us as good. We may also repress the fact that we lied so that *we* can continue to believe in our goodness. That's what forms the shadow—feelings and behaviors that we have and do that we don't want to admit having.

We develop a myth about ourselves to live by and try to ignore parts of ourselves that fail to support that myth. In our culture, traits like sexuality, rage, jealousy and selfishness get suppressed, and they form the elusive, perverse and mercurial shadow. We may try to block its subversive influence, but it is an inextricable part of our emotional lives. It lives, and it seeks expression.

Exercise

Read this story and respond to it in your notebooks.

A young man worshipped the heroic image of John Wayne. He was convinced that he, too, had the ability to act as Wayne did in many of his movies. He developed a fantasy about himself in which he had the opportunity to act in a multitude of heroic ways, and he even asked a few close friends to call him the Duke (Wayne's nickname). Then one day he accompanied a friend to a large city. They were walking down a street, talking about a movie they had just seen. Suddenly, they were confronted by muggers. "The Duke" took off running, leaving his friend behind. That day he realized he was too cowardly to be the person he believed himself to be.

For your writing, think of a time in your life when you discovered something that you had not realized was part of your personality. Describe the circumstances and reflect (in writing) how you think it's possible that you may not know parts of yourself.

If you're in a group, listen to the vignettes of three other people, and discuss what this indicates about who we are.

Then add a paragraph about how this quirk in our self-awareness can affect our goals for finding our bliss.

The shadow content of our lives contradicts who we think we are. We block out that which makes us feel inferior so that we can see ourselves the way we want to be seen. We develop a sort of authority in the "light"—what is visible—and dislike anything that challenges it, which the shadow does. The tension between shadow and light provokes anxiety and we do what we can to ignore it, but it never goes away. Thus we associate fear with our shadow sides.

In Russell Bank's novel, *Affliction*, we find an extreme example of this contradiction. The narrator is a man whose brother attempts to deal with the violence he endured from his alcoholic father by denying it, but here and there the "affliction" springs out. He insists he will never be like his father, but he gets upset at his daughter, who lives in fear of his outbursts; he also acts out in rage and on the brink of harming a friend, catches himself just in time. He wants to believe he will not *really* harm anyone—that he is not like his father—but the rage and tendency toward violence lie right below the surface, ready to strike. Finally, it all breaks loose, with tragic results for numerous people. Shadow energy, deeply repressed, builds into a force that will have its way.

Less intense but just as instructive, is the story, *A Simple Plan,* written by Scott Smith. Three men find a bag containing several million dollars and decide to keep it until they can determine who the owner is. The wife of one of these men, given this discovery as a hypothetical moral dilemma, insists that if she were to find such a bag, she would turn it in. She only proves that she does not know herself very well. As greed and deception unravel their lives, the wife proves to be the most devious in finding ways to keep the money. Her repressed shadow side ends up motivating behavior that she would never have recognized had she not been exposed to the actual situation.

Does this mean that our shadow side is bad, evil or something to be feared? No. I used the above examples precisely because they are so shocking. They make us see how important it is to pay attention to who we are. Most of our own experiences are more mundane, but are just as important to bringing awareness in our progress toward bliss. The more we deny something that is true of ourselves, the more likely it is that our behavior will be adversely affected by it. Repressing or denying psychological energy makes it contract into a more intense field. It is a living part of ourselves, seeking expression and attention just like any other part of the ego. The more we pretend it does not exist, the more it will insist on attention in some form. It's just like the shadow that tags along behind us on a sunny day. Running from it, stomping on it or pretending it's not there will have no effect. It will follow us wherever we go.

Since the shadow is primarily made up of psychological energy, it is important to realize that it also can contain surprising potential. I knew a man who was raised in a home where strong emotion of any kind was disapproved of. Thus, he learned to suppress such wonderful emotions as enthusiasm and joy. They were stuffed into his shadow. Only by acknowledging that our dark chambers conceal a prism of energies can we discover the riches within. "One does not become enlightened by imagining figures of light," Jung pointed out, "but by making the darkness conscious."

★ Mining the Shadow ★

We can find within the shadow deeper self-revelation and greater personal power. If we are willing to examine what's there, we can find ways to stop these traits from blocking us and ways to integrate this potency into our conscious lives. As Jung surmised, the psyche craves wholeness. The larger Self is connected to both chaos and order, and it cannot be totally brought into the light or demystified. Our unconscious potential is part of who we are.

William Styron, who wrote *Sophie's Choice*, also wrote a memoir about his difficult bouts with alcoholism and depression called *Darkness Visible: A Memoir of Madness*. He met up with his shadow in a rather intense way that nearly cost him his life, but once he faced it and worked with it, he found a greater appreciation for life and for his talent.

In 1985, he began to lose lucidity. He felt helpless, floundering about in the experience of dislocation and disorientation. Whatever was happening to him was eroding a lifelong belief in his psychic health, showing him that below the surface was something else altogether. He became depressed, but he refused to get treatment. He'd always been able to handle his life, so he tried to ignore the symptoms. Finally, it got so bad that he had to seek help. He attributed the entire episode to the fact that, after forty years of abusing alcohol (presumably to aid his creativity), his body chemistry had radically changed and he could no longer tolerate the substance. As he struggled with the depression, he felt like he had split into two selves, one that dispassionately watched while the other disintegrated into inertia. He came very close to committing suicide, but was helped by a friend who had gone through something similar.

When he recovered, Styron looked back over his own work and noticed how his shadow side—this self-destructive depression—had been there all along: Suicide was a persistent theme in his books. He figured he had suppressed some intense emotions that had developed from unresolved mourning. While he was growing up, his own father had been hospitalized for depression and his mother had died when he was thirteen. He used his books to try to reconcile death with immortality. The "madness" that finally surfaced after he turned sixty had been part of him for a long time.

For our purposes, this story shows several aspects of the shadow, particularly how it relates to finding our bliss.

1. Often we don't (or won't) see those things inside us that may one day make themselves known in some drastic way. It's better to practice self-examination.

2. Shadow material is often complex, a double-sided archetype that gives off both a positive and negative charge. It embodies contradiction, uniting life and death. Offering a fuller experience of passion, marginality, surrender and power, the shadow stretches and challenges us. It ex-

tends to us the energy of our unlived lives. It is not a problem to be solved, but an inner entity to be engaged as part of us.

3. The shadow can feed creativity. Styron's unresolved issues helped him to create masterpieces. While they nearly disabled him, once he understood what was at work, he was able to channel them toward another creative realm—a nonfiction book about his experience with self-awareness at the deepest levels.

★ Shadowboxing ★

Looking at values, sources of approval and sources of personal identity reveal those things that are most meaningful to us. They also hold clues about just how we may prevent ourselves from using them toward self-fulfillment. The subconscious strives toward wholeness. Working through those fears can show us our gifts and free us for peak moments. Often, however, we don't see them.

Exercise

Read the following example of a person with a blind spot and list some creative ideas that you believe might help him to realize how his actions undermine his beliefs about himself.

Stephen denied that he ever felt rage against anyone. He presented himself as a good Christian man who wanted to be generous to others. However, whenever someone crossed him, he found a covert way to make that person pay for what they did. For example, when a boss criticized him, he went into her garden one night and cut the heads off her prize roses. One time when his mother failed to come through for him when he was ill, he started a nasty rumor about her. He was constantly setting one friend against another. Instead of admitting and dealing with his rage, he allowed it to come out in quick, harmful acts that he dismissed as insignificant. His intention was to go into the ministry because

After writing down your ideas, read this similar story that offers more context:

Sandra believed that she was a generous person and devoted friend. She urged people to call her or visit her, but whenever someone took her up on her invitation, she found reasons why she could not see them. Even worse, she would tell someone to drop by at a certain time and then just not be home. If someone called at an inconvenient time, she would pretend she was ill—sometimes seriously ill. Although she insisted that she would do whatever it took to develop a friendship, her actions indicated that she was fairly blind to how uncommitted she really was and how little regard she had for others.

I met her mother and when I described Sandra's behavior, the woman said, "She's always been like that. I've had to lie for her so often. And her brother is exactly the same way. They both do this, and I have no idea why or where it came from!"

Children aren't hardwired for these types of behaviors. My guess was that if both of her children avoided friendships, but failed to see what they were doing, they learned that behavior from the same source: the very person who insisted she did not know where this behavior came from (she was blind to *her own* behavior). In fact, after talking to her further, I soon learned that she tended to be reclusive, although she had been pressured since childhood to be hospitable. It seemed that she had developed a facade to please those who were pressuring her, but when she actually had to perform, such as having someone over for dinner, she withdrew. And she was surprised to see this same behavior in her children! Of course she would be surprised since she didn't see the same contradiction in her own approach to people. Her children were acting out their mother's pattern, having watched and absorbed it since childhood.

Looking at Stephen and Sandra, who present similar cases of contradiction between their self-beliefs and their behaviors, you can probably see that this contradiction is more complicated than it seems at first. To simply tell either of these people what they are doing fails to address the unconscious roots. Sandra most certainly grew up with this split between who she is and who she thinks she is. Stephen may have the same problem.

The difficulty for both is that they want to work with people. Sandra believed her calling was to get involved in social work in some manner. Since she had convinced herself that she wanted to help people, she could not see how her behavior said, "I want people to stay away from me." If social work is indeed her bliss, then she will need to work through her blind spots so she can see how she might sabotage herself. Failing to recognize how this inner contradiction might hinder her is like my story: Had I not realized through some reflective psychological work that I had this fear of financial insecurity (which was a pattern in my own family), I might have allowed it to motivate me to withdraw from my bliss.

A lot of us develop a story about ourselves that we want others to believe but which belies our true nature. This comes from living in a family or culture that pressures us to conform rather than celebrate our unique identities. Unfortunately, we are all prone to developing the kind of blindness that Sandra, her family and Stephen exhibited.

Nevertheless, there is a positive side to the shadow self. It is not just negative traits that get passed on. Anne Lamott describes the home in which she grew up as a quiet place where reading rituals prevailed. Her father was a writer and in the evenings, he went to the couch, her mother sat in the easy chair and she and her brothers found their own readings posts. They grew up absorbing this atmosphere, growing used to it and developing their comfort zone there. Lamott eventually became a best-selling author, in large part, I would say, because immersion in words and deep concentration were daily habits from childhood. Because they were part of her routine, she did not necessarily see how they influenced her, and yet they did influence her quite profoundly. They became part of her, a blind spot of a sort that fed into her future career.

Shadowboxing means taking a good, hard look at our family legacy and at the traits we've developed that don't necessarily contribute something to our lives. My insecurity away from structure and Sandra's mixed messages are examples of such traits, but there are many others. In the next chapter, I'll describe a technique that I have used to help others with this kind of awareness. Since our shadow is something we prefer not to know about, it's tricky to get people to see it. There is a way, but it involves sneaking up on it from behind.

First, however, I want you to do more exercises that will give you several different ways to reflect on the concept of the shadow and how it plays out in your own life. Remember, those parts of yourself that you resist or cannot see may work against you in your pursuit of bliss. The more you become aware of behavior patterns that signal an unconscious motivation, the more likely it is that you can examine them for their potential to block you.

Exercises

1. Write a page about how you discovered that a belief you had developed about yourself had failed you in some way. Describe the situation in detail and then try to determine what you learned about yourself through the experience.

2. Pinpoint two examples of a cultural shadow and discuss the rituals we have developed to keep it at bay. (*Hint:* Look at movies that have characters who kill or destroy, or that paint some character trait as "bad." You can see implicit judgements with the cultural patterns presented in art, film and literature.) Then come up with a more creative response.

3. Describe how these cultural shadows may have affected you.

★ Our Personal Shadow ★

The shadow material of our culture, reflected in film, art, literature, political conditions and ideologies, influences how our personal shadow forms. So does our family life, as well as the kinds of relationships, including friendships, to which we gravitate. To get a better sense of your personal shadow, do the exercise below.

Exercise

Answer the following questions:

* What traits do you dislike in other people?
* If you've ever really hated someone, try to determine why.
* With what kinds of people or groups do you feel the most comfortable?
* What kinds of people frighten you?
* If you have siblings, over what kinds of things do you have conflicts?
* What kinds of people do you completely avoid?
* What traits would you find most difficult to admit to being part of your personality?
* What circumstances would make life seem like it was not worth living?
* Imagine how a person you know but whom you dislike would evaluate you. What would that person say about your traits?
* Is there a type of person with whom you tend to get involved,

much to your chagrin in retrospect? If so, look at the patterns and describe the type of individual.

* Have you ever impulsively done something that didn't seem like you at all? If so, describe it.
* Over what kinds of faults do you get angry?
* What kinds of situations most humiliate you?

Now look over your responses to these questions and see if there are any patterns.

Here is one more exercise to try: Use your imagination to create a character based on those traits that you despise or that make you angry. Put yourself in dialogue with that person and write down whatever you learn about your own reactions.

Typically, those things inside of you that you wish to ignore or suppress will surface in your reactions, especially negative reactions. If someone's behavior really annoys you in any exaggerated way, you can bet you're looking into a mirror and not liking what you see.

★

The next chapter offers a technique that locates our shadow traits through an indirect manner, using our bodies to develop and deepen our self-awareness.

five

DOUBLE REFLECTION

★

In the 1990 film, *Mermaids*, starring Cher and Winona Ryder, a young woman tries to set herself apart from her family. It's the sixties, and her mother is a flamboyant, rebellious woman who runs from every relationship that gets serious. In the past fifteen years, she has moved eighteen times, and her daughters, Charlotte and Kate, are tired. They want some stability. Charlotte, the older girl, desperately wants to be a nun and to enter a convent, ignoring the fact that she is Jewish. She believes that her desire to change her identity proves how much unlike her mother she is. However, it proves the opposite. Like her mother, she tries to run away from who she is, but since she is shifting her identity psychologically rather than physically moving from place to place, she believes she is not repeating her mother's patterns. She is so insistent that she not be mistaken for her mother that she cannot see how like her mother she actually is—she exhibits the same pattern in a different way.

When I first saw this movie, I was struck by the subtlety of that kind of denial. I *felt* it and knew I had done something similar. Yet had I not seen the movie, I might never have come to that realization. It was not just a matter of watching the film and thinking about it. I actually had to feel the impact of seeing myself in the character. This is a deeper type of reflection—a *double* reflection. It happens in therapy a lot, especially when imagery and stories are used, but few people grasp it beyond the initial feeling and use it for deeper self-awareness.

Exercise

If you can, think of a situation in which a movie or book, or even some story you heard about someone else, affected you in such a way that you felt as if it were about your own life. Write down what that was like and include any reflections you had about it at the time. Also include what you think about it now.

Since you are interested in living your life in the most spiritually attuned manner, you can benefit from the technique described in the following section. It will help you begin to become aware of what may be hindering you in your path towards bliss.

★ DOUBLE REFLECTION ★

It was the Danish philosopher, Soren Kierkegaard, who first used the phrase "double reflection" to describe the act of enhanced awareness that I'm introducing here. This idea refers to the intuitive sense we have of our inner selves that we experience in brief flashes, as I did when watching that movie. This is an advanced notion, a step beyond ordinary self-reflection, and it's a much more subtle way to assess blind spots. Although it may occur sporadically in everyday life, once you understand its function, you can actually use it in a more directed manner.

This concept is part of many self-assessment techniques. It is about our unique and personal subjective experiences. It's the individual way in which we perceive our world and form concepts about reality.

There is no clear division between our outer and inner experiences; they tend to blend together in the same way that values and moods affect your perspective on any given day. Let's say you're pretty good at playing tennis. You look forward to meeting other players for a match and develop your skill with great eagerness. However, suppose you go through a losing streak. It seems that nothing you do turns out right. The idea of a match now is much less enticing. In fact, you might do whatever you can to avoid it. As you lose your feel for the game, you grow less enthusiastic about it. Simple shifts in your experience can affect your attitudes. That's a bit of how you move toward double reflection—recognizing how your perception of something is influenced by changing experiences. It's about *who* you are *in* your experiences.

Whenever you see a film with several other people and you each express a different opinion about it, you get a glimpse of your subjective self; you see that who you are in your experience is unique. You and your friends may share the same language and common cultural experiences, but you absorbed the film in individual ways.

Let me give you a simpler example. I once owned a couch that was getting worn out, but it suited my purpose of allowing me to sit and watch television. I didn't really notice it much beyond its utility. Then I invited someone over who I knew would look at everything in the room with a critical eye, and suddenly I saw things about that couch I'd never noticed before: a worn spot on the arm, a spring coming through, a hole in the cushion. I couldn't believe I sat on that couch nearly every day and simply did not see these flaws—at least, not until I saw them through someone else's eyes. Thus my values—not caring that much about what I sat on—blurred the appearance of that couch, and someone else's values brought it into focus. Recognizing those values gave me a new way to see it. The holes were always there, but it took some reason for them to become important to me before I could see them.

The idea of reflecting on your subjective experiences gets even more complicated. You cannot observe your inner experiences—your moods and feelings—in the same way that you might look at a couch. Your experiences are far too complex and elusive for that. Unlike an object that sits there, your experiences are dynamic and you can only be aware of a small bit of them at any given moment. So the point is not to observe them, but to become aware of them in your body as they are occurring.

Which brings us to the body and its very important function in our awareness and development of intuition. Our blind spots have a lot to do with our bodies, and being able to discover them means finding a way to experience our bodies reflectively.

★ Body Memories ★

In the 1700s, French philosopher René Descartes proposed that the mind and body were separate from each other. Today, it's a common idea. Essentially, Descartes said that the body takes up physical space and the mind does not, so they must be different types of substance that somehow interact. His logic wasn't that great and today many scholars criticize his arguments. Nevertheless, this view of our nature has become firmly entrenched in our culture. We need to understand what it is and why it is not true before we can work with double reflection as a tool for bliss.

This separation of mind and body has divided professionals into specializations that miss the larger picture. Physicians have mostly attended to the mechanics of the body, and psychologists or priests have claimed the mind and/or soul. Unfortunately, that has come to mean that treatment in one area can hinder or negate treatment in the other, or even affect it adversely.

Recent work in some areas of medicine indicates that the mind and body work together as a unit. Even if some part of the soul exits the body at death and continues to exist in a spiritual form, that does not negate how intimately linked it is to the body while in the physical realm.

Dr. Candace Pert, research professor in the Department of Physiology and Biophysics at Georgetown University Medical Center, is one of the pioneers in this field. Her work since 1972 is documented in her book, *Molecules of Emotion: Why You Feel the Way You Feel.* She has also written numerous articles on the way the mind and body function together and what her findings mean for our identities and experiences.

According to Pert, the chemicals in our bodies form an information network that links emotional experience with physiological systems. Accordingly, certain emotions become physically encoded into our cells, forming what she calls our "bodymind." This gives a scientific basis for intuition or "gut feelings," and explains how certain anniversaries bring back "felt" memories. Thus, not only can we better understand what this is all about, but once our knowledge advances, we can even enhance some of our body-based emotional abilities—particularly awareness and consciousness.

If it is true, as it seems to be, that our emotions are chemically based and controlled by an information system that is dynamic, flexible and adaptable, then we can think about our emotions as part of our bodies, and our bodies as having a part in our emotional states.

A vivid metaphor for this concept is the phenomenon known as the "phantom limb." Once a limb or other body part is removed, there is a common experience among amputees who feel that the limb is still in place and even have sensations such as pain. There is no real sensory input because no limb is there, but the feeling that it is still there is strong. A large percentage of amputees report quite vivid experiences, including ones with limbs that were removed decades earlier. Even those people born without limbs, who have never felt what it was like to have that arm or leg, report the sensations. Quite often the phantom limb feels more real—or at least more present—than the actual limbs did.

The most common sensation reported among this population is phantom pain, such as burning, cramping, pressure and itching. If a person without an arm is walking, it will feel as if the arm is swinging in the proper rhythm. One man reported that, after the amputation of his leg, he could feel his toes "clawed over," burning and red. And some people who scratch the empty air where the "limb" is missing report that the sensation eases.

No one knows the cause of this, although theories include such things as evidence of an astral body or neuronal firing in the stump (although neurosurgery often does not eliminate the sensation).

A better theory involves body images—or what I call body memories—which are grounded in the way the brain directs the cells. In the absence of genuine sensation from a limb, the brain continues to operate under the body image programming. To shift the feeling, the body image must be reprogrammed in some way, such as with hypnosis or drugs. It seems that perception has a lot to do with how the brain directs things rather than about external stimulation.

The idea, then, is that our bodies cocreate our perception with our experiences. How we physically and emotionally process the world has a lot to do with who we are, and it also contributes to our sense of identity. Thus, it makes sense to get to know your body and its response to the situations in which you find yourself. Physical sensations often provide clues about types of emotional processing. In that case, you can better understand who you are within your experiences.

Find a place to sit quietly. You will not be writing while you do this, but you will want to write about it immediately afterward. You might ask someone you know to write for you as you experience this exercise. The point of the exercise is to feel yourself in some situation.

Listen to your body and ask yourself how you're feeling today. Then get more specific and ask yourself what contributes to that particular state. For example, if you're not feeling so great today, try to determine what is bothering you. Pinpoint a feeling as specifically as you can.

Try to remain detached and feel where in your body this emotion is most forceful. Be as present to it as you can, even if it bothers you. Don't think about it or analyze it; just feel it. Then see if it is connected to other situations that bring out this same feeling, even things from your past. If several feelings emerge, try to focus on the primary one.

Try to name it or at least find a descriptive word for it. Wait a moment as you try this word on to see if it's right. If not, try again. Once you have the right word, stay with it so that you will be familiar with it the next time around. Then break away and write down what you experienced.

Next step: Imagine this same feeling in someone else who comes to talk to you about it. Describe what it is like to view the feeling from the other person's point of view. Imagine giving that person advice about the feeling and then imagine what it would be like for you to receive such advice. Describe how it affects you physically. Be specific.

Moving back and forth like that ought to give you a better

sense of who you are in your experience—how you might be similar to others but also unique. Retain some sense of this exercise, particularly as it relates to using your feelings as signals that you're moving in the right or wrong direction regarding your bliss. The more awareness of your experience you can achieve, the better you will be at detecting when you are or are not following your bliss.

★ Set Points ★

Now let's remain focused on the body and include one more thing: an understanding of our emotional "set points."

A set point is the idea that we have a favored physical state, such as a body weight. According to this idea (and many people trying to lose weight will attest to its accuracy), the body has a genetic code that decides its ideal weight. It doesn't read charts put out by insurance companies or doctors' offices. It reads its own genetic inheritance and moves naturally in that direction. That is, our bodies have their own weight set points, regardless of what society tells us they should be. When we try to lose weight, our bodies resist. When we succeed at losing weight, our bodies make us even hungrier in order to put those pounds back on. It might raise its set point to avoid the risk of going below its natural homeostasis, such as might occur in a natural environment when the food supply is dwindling.

Another type of set point involves our habits. For example, if you always place your toothbrush in a certain position relative to the bathroom sink and then go someplace where you cannot put it in the same position, you'll find yourself reaching where you're used to finding it, even if you know it's not there. That is a body memory, setting itself to go through the same motions each time you are in a certain situation.

Yet you can change such habituated behavior. If you're

used to getting up at 7:30 A.M. and want to change that to 6:30 A.M. so you can start jogging before work, you have to make that change every day for at least three weeks (the time that many people consider it takes to develop a behavior into a habit). The first few mornings will be difficult because your body is used to getting up at 7:30. However, if you force yourself to get up at 6:30 without fail, you will soon find it easier (perhaps not easy, but not as difficult as the first attempts) to do. You can change your set point, although not without effort. Your body "remembers" when you do certain things on a daily basis.

Now apply that concept to your emotional life. You grew up in a home in which there was a defined emotional climate, such as chaos, depression, tension, comfort or energy. Each member of your family—the parts of the whole—processed and contributed to that emotional climate in an individual way. For example, in a depressed home, some of the members may allow that emotional tone to penetrate their own psyche and then develop depression as their natural state. They would have to work hard or take stimulants of some kind to change the set point that develops in them. Other family members may resist the depression and overcompensate by developing a more excitable personality. Nevertheless, they will still resonate to that set point of depression that is part of the larger group, and when they grow up, they might end up being attracted to depressed people.

In any event, your home life had an effect on your emotional set point. It's important to become aware of your body and how it responds emotionally before you can effectively learn the process of double reflection.

Exercises

1. Look over this list of statements and write a brief response to each one in terms of how it feels as a description of you. If

you're doing this exercise in a group, have each person share what they have written about two items that the group selects.

"There is a plan for my life and I can find it."

"My goals are achievable."

"I trust my instincts."

"When I know what I want, I follow through."

"When I learn something about myself that is difficult to hear, I face it."

"I get involved with people who seem to have the same issues."

2. Now think of someone you know well and imagine how that person might respond to the same statements. Then compare what you wrote about yourself with what you imagined someone else would say, and think about the differences. Write a brief essay on what you learned. What's important is not the content of what you wrote, but how different your response might be from someone else's. One person might say that she does not trust her instincts very well and that's why she has trouble initiating a change in her life, while another might feel that her instincts are the only reliable guides in her life. It is not important who is correct. It's only important that you see how you respond in contrast to how others respond because that will provide information about your subjective experience.

3. Write a horror story. Then analyze it for what makes you afraid. Ask someone else to analyze it and compare what that person said with what you said. Once again, you're looking for the different ways that people respond to the same material.

4. Imagine facing a new job or having to learn a complicated new skill. Describe what this would be like for you and how you would overcome your anxiety. Compare the steps that you might take to those that someone else offers. Think about why you made the choices you did instead of the choices that the other person made. This, too, will give you some idea of how you have developed differently from other people. (It might be as simple as, "My father did it this way." Alternatively, it might be that you learned something from a difficult experience, and you changed how you did things.)

5. This exercise works best in a group but can still be effective when done on an individual basis. Write your response to this exercise in its entirety.

Imagine yourself in a hallway. Describe it.

Now move through the hallway and describe what you see.

You come to a set of stairs. Describe them.

Take the stairs to a doorway. Describe it.

Go through the door and into a room. This is your room, the room of your fantasies. It can be anything you want. Spend some time describing in detail what this room looks like and how you would furnish it. Only when you are finished should you look at the questions that follow.

If this exercise is done in a group, spend some time allowing each person to describe their rooms and then answer the questions below.

If not done in a group, see if you can get a friend to do this same exercise and then compare notes. What you can learn about yourself is determined from the way you filled in the details in contrast to the way someone else did. Avoid thinking about what something means on an objective level. For example, if you had a long hallway and someone else describes a short one, there is no definitive interpretation over why you have two different responses. A long hallway versus a short one, or going up the stairs instead of down means only what it says about you, and you are the one who should interpret that. Like dream imagery, what you describe has a context—you and your life story. An image in your dream, such as a snake, does not mean the same thing in another person's dream. You dreamed it because it means something to you.

With that in mind, answer the following questions about your fantasy:

Was your hallway long or short? Dark or light?

Did it have windows or doors, or nothing?

Was it made of brick, concrete, plaster, wood or something else?

Did you move through it slowly or quickly, by walking or running or flying?

What were the stairs like? Did you go up or down?

Was the door open or closed, or was there even a door? What was it made of?

Was there a door handle? What was it like? Was the door locked or unlocked?

Was your room small or large, with or without windows? Were there any pets in it? Any friends? Did it have a kitchen? A balcony? Plants? Statues? Paintings? Music? A large-screen television?

What can you learn about yourself from this room, especially by comparing it to what someone else has written? Look at the patterns of your responses and think about what they reveal. For example, a person might describe a long, empty hallway, carpeted and filled with bright light. He glides through it as if flying and goes up the stairs and through an open door into a room with a high ceiling, lots of space, no clutter and many windows. It has a large double door that leads to a spacious balcony overlooking the ocean. Do you feel the freedom that his vision expresses? Examine your own imagery in terms of how each part connects with the others.

Now that you have seen these questions, would you change anything? Can you learn something from the fact that you do or don't want to change it?

It should be clear by now that self-knowledge often comes from paying attention to things we don't normally notice, particularly our feelings and our bodies. We often assume our perspective is the way everyone else sees the world, and when we become mindful of the fact that we process things in our own subjective way, we develop the ability to know ourselves better in our uniqueness. The better we know ourselves, the better we can read how we respond to situations. We may also develop more confidence in our decisions, which is an important part of directing our lives toward what we really want.

Remember that this is a technique. It is not one of the stages of bliss, but will prove to be useful as you move into the next two stages: assessing your strengths and weaknesses.

Following is a list of useful ways to find out more about your blind spots. You can write these down if you want or talk about them in a group setting. Pick at least two to add to your notebook:

1. Look at family patterns in those members of your family whom you can observe. Often we do things automatically and don't realize it, such as laughing in the same way, carrying tension in the same part of our bodies, or having a tendency to be negative about new situations.

2. Learn to read your dreams, which I will say more about in chapter five.

3. Look at your patterns in significant relationships. People generally move toward their comfort zones. What are your comfort zones regarding the kind of people you prefer to be with?

4. Notice the similarities in the things you resonate with. For example, I like Beethoven, Dostoevsky and other artists for their intensity. I have a friend who will only read novels that are best-sellers because she needs the affirmation of so many other readers. Another friend of mine prefers Celtic music, light romance films and meditating on serene landscapes.

5. Examine yourself in a crisis. Think of how you react. Do you expect someone else to take over? Do you immediately know what must be done? Do you withdraw and hope it goes away?

6. Examine your effect on others: How do they treat you and what do you think they say about you when you're not there?

You'll learn other ways to find out more about your blind spots in the following chapters. Don't lose sight of the fact that the process of bliss is either hindered or facilitated by your psychology. The more you can develop insight about who you are, what resources you possess and how you feel any and all of that in your body, the more focused will be your pursuit of what you want. Double reflection is more attuned to a full experience of who you are in the ways that you respond and react than simple self-awareness exercises tend to get at. It brings in your body awareness, too. The more experienced you become at reading your physical responses, the better you'll be at noticing signals that indicate when you may be motivated by something in a blind spot or body memory.

With that said, let's get back to bliss.

six

Bliss Blockers

✶

When we neglect parts of our personality, we fail to notice that they can hinder us in finding and following our bliss. There are already enough external hindrances to self-awareness, such as meeting deadlines, balancing numerous tasks or meeting the demands of a family. Just making time to be self-reflective can be a real challenge. However, the things that hold us back are the very things to which we need to attend. These are the traits that double reflection is designed to assist you with.

Exercise

In the next section is a list of the most common mental blocks that get in the way of moving toward bliss. As you read through this list, try to identify those that seem most relevant to you and keep track of your reflections in your notebook. Highlight at least three that may be your personal stumbling blocks. It might help to recall what people who are close to you have said in regards to a behavior or pattern that you did not notice you had. You may also think about how strongly you react to these traits in others—a sure signal of shadow material.

We often stop ourselves from entertaining new ideas or trying out a new direction because we think we'll fail and want to avoid that at all costs. We think that if we have no track record, we can't possibly do well because there's no verification of our abilities. It's easier to stick with what we know, what we've already had success at, even though it's not satisfying to us or resonanting with us. Staying with the familiar, however, prevents us from discovering and developing new talents. It may take a leap of faith before confidence sets in, but it's important to determine if fear is holding us back.

bliss

BLISS

BLOCKERS

People tend to view failure as a dead end, a withering defeat, when it may be a way to sort out whether or not something is right for you. You have to take the risk and learn what doesn't work in order to get on with what does. All successful people have experienced setbacks. However, rather than view themselves as losers who failed, they simply recognize that they have to start over and do something in a different way. Apparent failure can be turned into a step toward success.

The flip side of the fear of failure is the fear of success, which can be just as debilitating and possibly more difficult to recognize or acknowledge. I once read about a person who wanted to work with language and idolized people who had written dictionaries. He set for himself the task of writing a new kind of dictionary, but each time he immersed himself in the project, he would lose interest (and money) because he'd think up yet another project that might work better. He never finished any of them. The man had potential but could not bring himself to manifest it in a way that would make him succeed. In that case, he knew his bliss—what most satisfied him—but he couldn't follow through with it.

Sometimes people develop this fear because they are afraid of surpassing their parents. Sometimes they just don't want the attention or new experiences that come with success. These same people are often prone to the next inner hurdle.

SELF-CRITICISM

This is a common one. Many people succumb to negative self-evaluations, which usually undermine rather than assist their efforts. I met a woman who wanted to move away from her secretarial position and become a photographer. I sent an opportunity her way to get a professional credit. She took the photos, but then felt they weren't good enough, so she took them all over again. Although her subject was completely satisfied and even paid her the money, she still obsessed over what she saw as flaws in the photos. Her incessant worry and self-criticism made her less and less attractive as someone to whom I would refer people, so she was actually undercutting her attempts to be professional. There was no doubt she had talent and passion, but her personal issues with imperfection got in her way.

This is a trait that many people possess. Don't skip over it too quickly.

NEED FOR CONTROL

A patient wrote this letter to his therapist:

> *Out of the evil much good has come to me. By keeping quiet, repressing nothing, remaining attentive and accepting reality—taking things as they are and not how I want them to be—by doing all this, unusual knowledge has come to me and unusual powers as well, such as I could never have imagined before. I always thought that when we accepted things they overpowered us in some way or other. That turns out not to be true at all, and it is only by accepting them that one can assume an attitude toward them.*

This discovery is true of bliss as well. Trying to control it rather than allow it to flow generally puts more tension into our lives, not less. Earlier I told the story of Peter, who tried to control the process of getting published to the point of deception and manipulation. Perhaps it made him feel better, but it got him no closer to finding his bliss. The need for control is another type of fear and often has to do with the feeling that letting go and allowing things to happen means being overwhelmed by them—literally drowning in them. There are certain things in life we *should* try to control because we need to take steps and make changes, but that's not the same as a more global type of control that arises out of deep anxiety.

The need for control is in all of us because we need security—some more than others. However, we need to recognize when our idea of control becomes illusory. There is a scene about this concept in the movie *Instinct*. It is about Dr. Powell, an anthropologist imprisoned for killing some men after they killed the band of gorillas that had befriended him. A young psychologist is trying to find out how this violence arose so he can get Powell out of prison. In the scene in question, he tries to prevent Powell from ending a session early. He claims that he is the one in charge. Powell deftly overpowers him and demonstrates that he could kill him in an instant. While holding the psychologist in a crushing armlock, Powell urges him to say what he has lost in that moment.

"Control," he chokes out.

"No."

Powell puts on more pressure but gives him another chance and he still gets it wrong. One more chance, Powell tells him, and if he doesn't get it right, his life is over. "What have I taken from you?" Powell demands to know.

The psychologist picks up a red crayon and writes, "My illusions."

That's the right answer, and Powell lets go. All along the young man has believed that because he's outside the prison and the one doing the interrogation, he was in control. It took a momentary lapse of awareness to show him that he was not, and in fact, much about what he believed he controlled in other areas of his life was illusory as well. It was as if Powell was a universal force that had tired of the brash attitude of one of its subjects and had decided to teach him a supreme lesson.

While most of us will never encounter that dramatic of a lesson, it's instructive to remember that we probably are less in control of our lives than we like to believe.

The irony of the need to control is how it can backlash and become an addiction. In that case, we actually *lose* control to our very need for it. Even worse, clinging to that need develops impatience, irritation and rigidity, all of which block the mind from exploration and discovery.

Nevertheless, we are not completely without control, and we need to find some balance between a sense of omnipotence that trips us up and a sense of helplessness that misleads us about our choices. It's important to remember that we have to make decisions and take the initiative, but these are not the same things as trying to control events that are beyond us.

MENTAL CONSTIPATION

This is something like writer's block. You get to a point where you no longer have ideas, or if you have them, you can no longer work on them. Sometimes that's a matter of merely going in the wrong direction with an idea.

In a novel I wrote, I joined two characters in a relationship, and suddenly I no longer wanted to write about them. I wasn't sure why, but it occurred to me that what I had lost in bringing those characters together was narrative tension. There was no place else to move the plot and no force to propel it. So I went back and rewrote the scene, setting up a hindrance to their getting together, and then went on to passionately write two hundred more pages.

Check out why you might be blocked and make some changes. Sometimes just a change in routines can loosen up the clog, or it may take getting some rest and relaxation. A bit more serious is the constipation that comes from a personality trait or need, such as the situation described in the following item.

A PERSONAL AGENDA THAT BECOMES RIGID

All of us like to view ourselves in a certain way; we develop a story that we like to believe and we tell it to others to get them to see us the way we prefer. There's nothing wrong with that, but sometimes our self-portrait leads us to deny certain things, as well as to want to become certain things, any of which can throw us off the track toward our bliss. When we firmly want something to be true, we may fight to make it so, and in doing so, lose our grounding.

For example, a celebrity typically has a team of people who work to develop an image that will be in that person's best commercial interests. A happy family life, solid values and a good work ethic are all part of the picture. Thus, when some reporter ferrets out a juicy item of gossip that goes against the image, the celebrity is upset. People might think of her other than the way she wants them to think, and then they might avoid or boycott her film, television show or product. She wants her carefully crafted image to be how others know her.

We can see parallels in our own lives. I once read a book written by a man who had lost his job as a college professor because he had failed to get tenure. He assumed that since he had a Ph.D., he'd eventually get hired at another school. He applied to a few and was rejected. He applied to more schools. Same story. Frantic, he sent out hundreds of applications all over the country. Each time, he failed to be offered a position. It seemed unthinkable to him that a man of his stature and education might have to take something less than a college-level job. However, after being unemployed for nearly a year and facing increasing debt, he soon had to admit this reality. There were no guarantees, despite the portrait he had developed about himself throughout his schooling, that he was on his way to bigger things. Yet when he did take a more menial job—that of a laborer—he learned some valuable lessons about life and how he had duped himself.

Sometimes life isn't as neat as the narratives we build. We need narrative for momentum, but we also need to realize when we've built into our self-portrait a resistance to the changes and demands of reality.

INERTIA

This can be anything from boredom to serious depression. If you often suffer from inertia, it's important to look at the conditions in which it occurs to check for patterns. (It may also be useful to check with your doctor.) If it's an occasional problem, then it may be a matter of feeling stagnant and not having direction. In that case, try to make some changes in your life to see if that breaks up the block.

One of the most common reasons for inertia—the inability to make a change—is what I call the Golden Handcuffs. You're in a job that's going nowhere or is terribly unsatisfying, and yet you cannot make the break because of the security that comes from a paycheck. Check this out in your family legacy. Was it something you were raised with? Earlier I mentioned the hairdresser who was urged toward a more lucrative field by parents who felt insecure with her desired direction. Fortunately, she was able to break away from that and follow her bliss.

I knew another young woman who did the guided fantasy through the hallway, room and stairs. She wanted to be an artist, but her parents persistently tried to discourage her from this career. When she mentally designed her "room," she made it round and to her dismay, found that she could not hang any of her own paintings. She had to rethink her ideas about what she wanted and wondered if a career in art was really as important to her as she had believed. She also wondered if she might have blocked herself from seriously pursuing it because her parents were so afraid for her. It was not long before she realized, thanks to her work with the fantasy, that her inability to know what she wanted had stopped her from going further, such as applying to art school. Inertia was closing in, so she did some work to find out what she really wanted and made plans to get moving on it.

REFUSAL TO BELIEVE THERE'S ANY NEED FOR SELF-EXAMINATION

Again, I refer you to William Styron's story. This is a smug attitude, according to him, that pretends that all is well and there are no imperfections in one's family life, relationships or life choices. One must wonder what that person is trying to hide, or what demons are simply too terrible to face. We all have blind spots and generally can benefit from a bit of self-examination. Males are more prone to this attitude than females, in part because they are taught to protect the family and to present a facade of strength. If you find yourself skipping quickly through this chapter as if it does not apply to you, I urge you to give it more thought. You may be falling into this very trap.

DEPENDENCY

I once heard a speaker on self-esteem mention something he had said to a patient when he had been a therapist: He knew when a patient was getting better when that person realized no one was coming.

"What does that mean?" his patient asked.

"It means that no one is coming to tell you how to live, to decide for you how to manage your life. You're on your own. No one is coming."

"But . . ." replied the patient, "you came."

"That's right," said the therapist. "And I'm here to tell you that no one is coming!"

I saved this one for last because it's one of the primary insights that a person must have. It's often referred to as the "existential moment." It's the time when you own your life, when you realize that you alone can make and are responsible for your decisions. Others can offer guidance, wisdom and practical assistance. Others may even hold certain powers over you. Yet it is you who decides how to accept, reject, interpret and apply those things. You can only direct your life toward its ultimate end when you recognize yourself as the one who gives meaning to whatever data comes at you, the one who filters it all through a unique perspective.

Since this is an important realization—blindness that may cause some real problems for your progress—make sure you try the exercise below.

Exercise

Write about how it feels to know that you alone are in charge of your life, despite the fact that you might not be in control of everything that happens. Include any ideas about future directions that this may give you.

To realize that no one is coming can be a rather scary moment. Responsibility can be a burden, especially when faced with the most important life choices. Yet mindfully maneuvering ourselves through life with an eye toward finding and fueling our bliss requires that we understand how essential our personal perspective is to all of this—and how we develop and maintain our perspective.

How do you become more aware of your habitual way of being in the world? How do you examine yourself? Think about the traits you wrote about in your notebook as you read through the following. (Please note: The traits listed on pages 84-91 are not the only possible hindrances. If you think of others more relevant to yourself, write about those in your notebook.)

bliss

BLISS

BLOCKERS

I once taught an all-day workshop for twelve people about the idea of bliss. The setting was the back room of a nice restaurant, decorated with plants and flowers that framed large windows. It was a good place for discussing our journeys through life.

However, one man in his mid-forties sat and listened with his arms crossed, his bearded face set in a grim expression. He remained quiet while others spoke and seemed to be passing judgment. He looked angry, and I began to wonder why he was even there. It was not like some required seminar in college. He was there because he chose to be, yet his resistant posture began to affect others, and it was clear that he was casting something of a pall on the sunny room. When we broke into small groups to work on an exercise, I went into his group and watched again as he remained outside the conversation. I asked him if there was something bothering him.

He was surprised. "No," he said, "I'm enjoying this."

Well, that surprised *me*. He certainly did not look as if he was enjoying himself. I asked him if he realized how tense and angry he looked. He shook his head, so I imitated his posture and asked him what that looked like to him.

"Am I doing that?" he asked.

Everyone in the group affirmed that indeed he was. He blushed, for the first time aware of the impression he was giving—an impression he did not want to give. That led to a discussion about how people often don't realize how their own posture or facial expressions, the way they walk into a room or the way they sit looks to others. In fact, one person said that he didn't see how we possibly could have such blind spots since we inhabit out bodies and must surely experience what we're doing. As he said this, he was tapping his fingers on the table in front of him. I asked if he was aware he was doing that as he spoke. He smiled, withdrew his hand and shook his head. "No, I guess I wasn't," he admitted. Point made.

If we have blind spots in our behavior, how do they form and how do we become aware of them in order to change them?

Typically, blind spots come from simply being so close to our experience that we're used to our behaviors and traits. What we do and how we do it become habits. Just like we don't notice our teeth until we have a toothache, we generally don't notice our habits until someone draws our attention to them. A blind spot follows you around, contributing to your behavior and perceptions, but you don't generally look at it.

The other reason we don't see facets of who we are is that we don't *like* certain traits, so we deny that we have them. Unfortunately, we still act them out, and others may suffer because our lack of awareness means lack of change. A friend of mine named Tina did not realize how assertive she was, but her behavior kept driving away potential friends. She saw herself as straightforward but failed to recognize the aggressive edge that accompanied her otherwise virtuous trait. Not seeing it, she continued to lose friends.

The same may happen for any of us, but instead of losing friends, we may lose opportunities, which in turn means we may be missing the track that will lead us to our bliss. Better to find out what others see and not allow those things to thwart us.

Someone else I knew who had come for therapy was in despair over the fact that she kept getting involved with men who cheated on her. I'll call her Laurie. Her latest relationship involved a man who liked to flirt. He considered this to be harmless fun that made him feel good. Laurie saw it as a way for him to keep his options open in case he found someone better, but in the meantime, he'd make do with her. She was distressed over his inability to see from her point of view; he was angry that she wanted to force him to give up something he perceived as a harmless diversion that in no way compromised their relationship.

The odd thing was, Laurie had met another man who was paying some attention to her. She loved the sound of his voice and the way it made her feel when he spoke to her. She had already lied to her boyfriend several times in order to sneak off to see this other man. Although she did not want this new development to rock the boat of her primary relationship, she thought it was okay for her to indulge in a little flirtation.

Now it seems like Laurie would see the obvious: She's doing exactly what her boyfriend is doing, yet she complains about him doing it. How does she dare to have such a double standard?

The answer is that she does not view their behavior as being the same. This is important to note, because many of us fall into this kind of self-deception. According to her, her boyfriend is "playing his options and stringing her along," while she is "merely having some fun with no intention of leaving her boyfriend." In other words, she can protect her sense of integrity by calling the same behavior two different things. She dislikes what her boyfriend is doing, so she cannot own up to the fact that she is doing it, too. Thus, she frames it differently so she can get away with being upset with him while excusing herself.

If we're honest, a lot of us can admit to having been

in similar situations. And sometimes our inability to see what we're doing is even more insidious than merely using the camouflage of language. When we use a trick of language to hide things about ourselves from ourselves, we can't work on them. When we can't work on them, they have the potential to undermine us.

One way to detect these kinds of traits is to think about what most annoys you in other people, as you did in the exercise above. It's likely that there is some manifestation of that trait in you, but you don't like it, so you don't see it. I dated a man who was the epitome of narcissism. He told me that several women he knew thought he looked arrogant, and he couldn't understand how they got such an impression. I wanted to say, "Well, maybe because you *are*." But I knew he wouldn't see it precisely because he refused to. As a result, he would continue to give that impression, much to his utter consternation.

Be warned: Self-examination for the purpose of self-awareness can show you things you may not want to see. However, the options are that (1) you will retain that trait or behavior when you fail to become aware of it, or (2) you can get into a position to change because you allow yourself to be exposed to something that's difficult to acknowledge. The behavior won't go away on its own. You either keep it or get rid of it, and only through awareness can you make a change.

★ BLISS AND THE SHADOW ★

It should be obvious by now that you may want to do or become something, but you may be the one blocking that goal. Those things about you that are hidden in your shadow as blind spots or absorbed attitudes and behaviors can sabotage any effort you make in trying to ascertain and then follow your bliss.

Exercise

1. Make a list of activities that affirm what you value.

2. Examine how much of your life involves these activities.

3. If you are not pursuing the things you want, what is hindering you?

4. Describe how it feels not to be doing those things.

5. Imagine ways to make those activities more central to your life.

6. Describe how it would feel to actually do some of those things mentioned in item 5.

★

Finding your bliss is about bringing into your life that activity that best brings out your potential and helps you realize the fullness of yourself. It's not necessarily about your life dreams, but those may be indicators of where you ought to be going. Once you get on the right track, opportunities should come your way. You'll be able to develop your skill into the experience of flow that yields your best and most satisfying work. However, this is not simply a matter of just making a choice. Finding your bliss often means working to find out more about yourself and figuring out how to get past some hurdles. In the following example, you can see this process at work in my own life.

One of the things I've learned about myself is that my bliss will involve learning, because nothing satisfies me as much as learning and nothing depresses me as much as being in a mentally inactive state. Although my career is that of a writer, I'm interested in other things that could guide it into more specific directions. Thus, in my mid-forties, I decided to return to graduate school.

My first task was to look over my options. Since I was interested in improving my writing, an MFA was a possibility. I was also interested in criminal justice and had recently been writing up criminal cases. In addition, I pondered a degree in business and even a paralegal course. There were a lot of potential directions, and I had to narrow them down.

Then I heard about a professional school in New York that offered a master's degree in forensic psychology. It meant I would have to commute, but when I got a catalog of the courses, I knew this was what I wanted to pursue.

However, I came up against a hurdle: anxiety over getting everything organized to go ahead and do this. It meant writing to various schools I had attended to get transcripts, finding former professors from years before to write recommendations and having to do all the other things required to matriculate. The easiest course would have been to forget it and be satisfied with my career. There were many days when that was tempting. But I also knew my tendency to remain right where I was, and each time I forced myself into a new arena, I was happy that I did. So I had a pattern and moving forward meant not only being familiar with what it was and how it could block me, but also developing a strategy to resist it when it did block me.

I signed up for the program and got the necessary papers to the school. Then it came time for class and I wondered what it would be like going in with these young students, especially after I'd already been a college professor for sixteen years. I had some qualms and wondered if I was doing the right thing. It meant spending a lot of money, commuting one or two days each week, taking time away from my career, doing homework again and committing myself to a program that could take as long as two-and-a-half years.

I had to take some time to feel what this was like for me. I did the body exercises mentioned earlier, comparing how it felt to go through with it against how it felt not to do it. The feeling I had in the latter option was one of suffocation and loss of momentum. That was more disturbing to me than the discomforts of all the arrangements and of actually being a student again. So I went for it.

From the first day, it was wonderful. I couldn't get enough. I went all the way through and never for one moment regretted it. So, for me, this was a sort of bliss—finding a track that felt right and kept me learning. It would also enhance my writing. I soon became a staff writer for a forensic psychology newsletter, contributed articles to a crime Web Site and changed the direction of my writing altogether. It was a process of sorting through what I wanted, looking at what might be blocking me, motivating myself to go through with what I wanted and then developing the discipline to keep going.

In the second part of this book, you will learn more about techniques to hone your personal traits into tools that will work for you as you move closer to discovering your life's path. To some extent, they depend on you doing the work from this first half, so if you've skipped over some things, I recommend you go back and do those exercises now. Then, move on to the next section.

Part Two

FLOWING INTO BLISS

★

seven

CREATING A SAFE SPACE

★

I had lunch with a woman in her early forties who told me that every time she moved, even when it meant moving from one state to another and changing a job, she did it because of a gut feeling she had. No matter how dramatic, she went with it. Once she simply left a job and went to a new state without even knowing what she was going to do, moving merely on the feeling that she ought to. It worked out and she's happy she made the move.

"You always trust your instinct?" I asked.

"Always," she replied. "It's never let me down. Each time I go with it, I never regret it. When I hear it but don't listen, that's when I get into trouble. It really doesn't fail me."

That would be my definition of feeling safe. When you believe you have an unerring sense of inner guidance and you follow it with the confidence that you will not be led astray, you have to feel very safe indeed.

Most of us, I presume, are not quite so secure with our feelings. We've been taught to look to external sources for affirmation and authority in our life decisions, especially when those decisions require major changes or investments. However, that is not necessarily a positive thing.

Before we can move into our bliss with complete confidence, we may need to reconnect with our inner authority. When we were children, older people probably questioned our ideas in an attempt to remold our thinking in a way that felt better to them. What they accomplished was to undermine our self-trust. I knew of one woman whose mother was so frightened of her imaginary playmate that she had a priest try to exorcise her! After that, she became suspicious of her own imagination, which later hindered her creative endeavors. It doesn't have to be that extreme, however, to make us begin to doubt ourselves, and for some, that doubt has an enduring effect.

"I remember that I really wanted to be a teacher," a man named David told me. "I loved school and my own teachers were so inspiring when I was growing up. But my father was concerned that I wouldn't amount to much if I pursued that profession, so he steered me toward computers and business management. He had me so convinced I didn't know what was best for me that I followed his plan all the way through college and halfway through a master's program before I realized how utterly unhappy I was. I actually had to go through therapy to find out that I wasn't living my own life. I also needed therapy to break away from my father's command, even though he had died and was no longer there to disapprove. His guidance left a deep mark on me and even now, as I pursue what I always wanted to do, I still feel guilty. Nevertheless, I know it's my bliss. I'm so happy doing this, and I only wish everyone could love their job as much as I love mine."

Once it gets rooted, self-doubt creeps into almost every area of our lives. If we think our opinion counts for nothing, then whenever a friend expresses a contrary idea, we might yield to him or her and forget about developing our own thinking on the subject. If we fail to stand up for ourselves in a relationship, we may become the object of abuse or belittlement. The same goes for our life plan. If we believe our bliss is to do something that others would believe ludicrous or impossible for us, then we're in a vulnerable position if we tend to defer to others.

To feel safe within ourselves, we must first believe in the authority of our own perspective and ideas. From small issues to large, we need to get comfortable with our own voice.

Exercise

1a. Read the following passage and write a response/reaction to it. Then have the members of your group or a couple of friends do the same. Read everyone's response out loud, and then defend your response wherever it diverges from that of someone else. Point out why you feel as you do. (You won't be able to develop confidence in your ideas unless you interact with others; this is one exercise that does not work in solitude.)

Richard Dodson, a pitcher for the New York Yankees, was put on the disabled list one summer to "work on his mechanics." His performance failed to improve until he decided to forget the mechanics and just go out and pitch the ball. That game was his best in months.

"It got to the point," he said, "where I was thinking too much before I threw a pitch. It's tough enough . . .without worrying about whether your leg is in the right position."

Clearly he needed to be mechanically prepared, but overfocusing on those mechanics only hindered his performance. He had lost his edge because he was thinking through what he should do in a piecemeal, step-by-step fashion. Too much attention to external mechanics can dull rather than sharpen the mind.

1b. After talking with others about your response to this piece, write in your notebook about how it felt to express and defend your opinion.

If you felt intimidated and uncomfortable, select a passage, book or movie you feel strongly about and try this again. Now defend your passion, and then write again about what that felt like.

If it was easier for you to select your own item to defend, repeat the exercise with another item, feeling what it's like to develop a position of your own and state it clearly to others. Pay close attention to your physical responses and learn to affirm those in similar positions.

If you still felt intimidated, then keep trying. It's important to believe in yourself if you want to face down the challenges of others that may arise when you actually discover and follow your bliss. Think of the man who became a teacher: If his father was still alive, he would have to find a way to tell his dad that he was going to teach no matter what. Even so, his father undoubtedly would have used tactics to dissuade him or make him feel inadequate. That's not uncommon when others believe they know what you should do with your life. Reclaiming your inner authority is an important step in reaching your bliss.

★ Self-Facilitation ★

As we get to know ourselves, we use those strengths that enhance our chances of achieving our goals. We learn to let go of hindering self-judgments that prevent us from believing in a dream. We take the first steps in trusting ourselves. We get used to the idea that blissful work has a spiritual side. We can use these principles to help us keep our perspective and confidence through the more difficult parts of career building.

The most important step—and perhaps the most difficult—is to feel safe within yourself. The best way to do that is by identifying traits that will help move you toward self-realization. Below, I list some traits that have shown up in the lives of those who have successfully followed their bliss. Note any that you feel you possess, as well as those that you need to work on.

Take the case of Tom Clancy. He started out as an insurance broker with a passionate interest in naval history. He wanted to write about it, and it seemed to him that the best format would be fiction. He completely immersed himself in the technology of submarines and produced *The Hunt for Red October*. It was masterful writing, but editors who read it could not figure out how to place it in any of their genres (for which book stores reserve shelf space). Undaunted, Clancy found a publisher of military books, which meant it would only get limited distribution and attention. However, President Reagan read it and gave it a high recommendation, which made it soar to the top of the best-seller lists, where Clancy has remained for all of his subsequent books, several of which have been made into high-profile movies. He single-handedly created a new genre, the techno-thriller. Because of his persistence in keeping a vision for himself, he managed to act on a possibility that no one else could see.

CAPACITY TO SELF-CORRECT

It's not easy to admit when you've made a mistake or taken a course that seems to be leading to a dead end, but sometimes you will do those things. Even the most successful people will tell you that they've gotten off course or made a bad decision. It's better to admit and correct it than to keep going out of defensiveness or pride. In fact, making mistakes helps you see the right course more clearly, so you should welcome mistakes as guides.

ABILITY TO REFRAME ADVERSITY

You discover the meaning of an event by the way you view it—and there's more than one way to perceive almost anything. One afternoon, after I had been teaching in an adjunct position for around ten years (and being depressed by it), I found out that the state had decreased funding to the university and my position had evaporated. Although it meant I would have no income, the first words that came to me were, "Now my life begins." I was afraid, certainly, and had no idea what might happen, but I finally felt free to look in a new direction rather than bind myself in the "golden handcuffs." What might have seemed like the end of the world to some was a new beginning to me.

TOLERANCE

This means developing flexibility. You can listen to others without feeling threatened, and thereby gain ideas you may not have thought of yourself. You can also work better with people on projects that require teamwork or partnership.

ABILITY TO SET GOALS

Many successful people have clear plans, even if they don't fulfill them. Ruth, a bank manager, has a five-year plan that she periodically revises. It doesn't matter to her if she achieves everything on her list. It only matters that she has made herself accountable to a plan. It's important to have some clarity about where you're going; goals can help with that, even if those goals change.

AN ALERT, EAGER MIND

No matter how tolerant, self-aware or flexible you are, you won't get far without enthusiasm and eagerness to move forward. Finding your bliss is not just a matter of deciding what you most like to do, but developing the psychological energy to do it in a sustained, committed manner. An alert mind can take an ambiguous situation and find momentum to make that situation, whatever it is, work for you. When you are alert, you're more likely to notice the fine details that elude a more lethargic mind, and you can take advantage of those points. I met an entrepreneur who was asked to financially support a capital venture. When the people in charge ran out of money and asked him for more, he took over the project. Since he was gambling with his own money and not someone else's, he was more alert to opportunities as well as to the potential pitfalls that the others did not see. He managed to turn their venture into a profitable enterprise, whereas they would have continued to lose money in the same arena.

ABILITY TO TAKE A RISK

The process of bliss quite often involves change, and change can involve risk—or at least the feeling that you're taking a risk. You might be leaving a cushy job to try something new, or you might be venturing into a field in which there is little security. If you tend to avoid risk, it's probably because it threatens your status quo. The thought of risk is often uncomfortable and even frightening. However, when you're taking a risk in the service of your bliss, you can think of it as a threshold toward your greater good. Monica, a woman I met, told me how she'd met another woman, Linda, on the Internet and how they began to talk about their mutual passion for exotic plants. The more they shared, the more it seemed possible to develop a business together, but the main hurdle was that they lived in different parts of the country.

Monica had just gone through a divorce and was trying to reorient herself. She wasn't sure she could make any more dramatic changes. However, Linda knew of a place she could rent for a reasonable price and offered to front the initial expenses of starting up a business. Still, Monica was not so sure this was a good idea. She hedged for a few days, but the idea of immersing herself in something she was passionate about, along with a friend who was there to support her, proved to be enticing. It was true that she didn't know Linda very well. Nevertheless, the offer nagged at her until she finally decided to go for it. She moved near Linda, and they started a business in exotic plants. There were some initial problem spots, but soon they got it rolling. Monica never regretted her decision to close the door on her old life and take up something altogether different.

MINDFULNESS

bliss

CREATING A
SAFE SPACE

This term was coined by Dr. Ellen Langer, who researched the differences between people who did things simply out of routine and people who were fully engaged in their tasks, even those that were routine. In one study, she found that elderly residents who were given the responsibility to make decisions about nurturing a plant were more active and positive than those who had no such project. Caring involvement and acceptance of responsibility are aspects of mindfulness. Sticking with routines, Langer found, not only restricts our thinking from going in creative directions, but can also dull our alertness in situations when we need to keep our eyes open. We engage in mindless behavior by thoughtlessly following instructions, going through the motions of a routine and failing to retain useful information because we weren't thinking about it. What mindful people say and do matters to them, and it makes a difference in the way they live their lives. It's a key trait for those interested in finding their bliss, because we need to develop caring attention and focus to avoid the blindness that comes with routine thinking.

ABILITY TO BE CHALLENGED

Some of the brightest people I have ever encountered were unable to admit that their ideas were open to challenge. I've even known those who were so caught up in their image of expertise that they spoke out authoritatively on subjects they had little or no experience with!

In Socrates' pursuit of truth, he never felt entirely "finished." Even if it seemed that he knew something about a subject like goodness or truth, he continued asking questions of everyone he encountered who also claimed to have knowledge about that subject—to the point of making himself a nuisance. Finally, the local politicians opted to get rid of him. Nevertheless, he honed his own moral life with the questions he asked, never imagining that he had arrived. If you adopt an attitude that you can always improve, then challenges will seem less like attacks and more like opportunities for self-examination and growth. Challenge is one way to continually upgrade your personal standards.

ABILITY TO REMAIN CALM THROUGH CHANGE

This takes you back to the Zen state of being inwardly relaxed, no matter what may be happening around you. You're grounded even as you move forward, so you can remain centered and confident. This is an inner discipline that shows self-control and a sense of direction. You'll learn more about the art of concentration, which is the basis for this ability, in another chapter.

Exercises

1. Go over the ten traits listed above and write about the top three that you feel you need to develop. Explain what you mean and come up with an experience or activity that might assist you.

2. If you think the type of activity that may be your bliss involves traits other than those on the list, write them down. Assess whether you need to develop those traits. Make some notes on how you might do this.

3. Do each of the following, allowing enough time to give a full response:

A. Describe a technique or ritual you use to minimize stress and find a sense of comfort. If you don't currently practice one, imagine what ritual or technique you might use toward this end. Describe it fully in your notebook.

B. Try to recall a dream you had in which you felt endangered and then safe again. What made you feel safe in the dream?

C. Imagine that you are doing what you believe to be your life's calling. Describe how it feels.

D. Now review these three descriptions. Are the feelings of safety you describe similar to the feelings you have when thinking about what you believe you are meant to do? Note the similarities, but also note where they might diverge. The exercise should help you determine whether you would actually feel safe doing what you believe is your bliss.

★ PRACTICAL BLISS ★

It's time to imagine yourself in your arena of bliss. Imagine what it would be like to be a writer, entrepreneur, surgeon or professional athlete, and describe how it feels. I've known people who have gone through several career preparations before they found the one that felt right and "safe" in terms of who they believed they were. One lawyer told me she had gotten two graduate degrees in separate fields: a Ph.D. in psychology and a J.D. in law. She had tried a few things in psychology, even teaching, but eventually became a defense attorney. "This is me," she said. "I feel right at home in the courtroom, and when I'm gone from it, I miss it."

Another lawyer told me he'd started out as a prosecutor because he loved the law, but when it came time to deal with criminals face to face, he found the whole thing unpleasant. He reoriented himself and went into civil law, where he felt very satisfied.

One of the best ways to determine what direction you might take is to assess your actual skills. You may find that while you want to be a professional basketball player, you lack coordination. Go through the exercise below and take a good, hard look. Once you've gained a sense of who you are through your skills, compare it to what's needed to follow your bliss. It may mean you need to get additional education or training, or that your current idea of bliss is more likely a dream and not something you will be able to do with satisfying results.

One of the best ways to know whether or not you should move toward a certain occupation is to go through a skills inventory. In your notebook, you might want to write down the entire list that follows or just include those skills you believe you have. It's important that you give yourself an honest evaluation. You don't have to prove anything to anyone, but if you list skills that you wish you had or want others to believe you have, it defeats the purpose of finding the path that feels most true to who you are.

1. Go through the skills inventory and put a check beside those skills you have or have had in the past, regardless of whether you do them as well as you want.

____ I'm organized	____ I'm good with animals
____ I'm a good listener	____ I'm physically coordinated
____ I'm intuitive	____ I'm good with languages
____ I like to analyze things	____ I can usually solve problems
____ I make decisions easily	____ I stick to decisions I make
____ I follow instructions well	____ I tend to take the lead in things
____ I'm good with children	____ I'm empathic with older people
____ I can delegate responsibility	____ I research thoroughly
____ I write clearly	____ I sense what people need
____ I can resolve disputes	____ I can make people laugh
____ I work well with others	____ I'm self-motivated
____ I'm disciplined	____ I can get people to cooperate
____ I'm a good instructor	____ I can concentrate for hours
____ I put people at ease	____ I get things done quickly

___ I can motivate others   ___ I finish what I start

___ I'm reliable   ___ I'm good at designing

___ I take criticism well   ___ I have musical talent

___ I'm artistic   ___ I meet deadlines

___ I can talk in front of others   ___ I'm good at planning

___ I like to brainstorm   ___ I get right to work

___ I adjust well to change   ___ I figure out how things work

___ I can take on multiple projects   ___ I help others with problems

___ I can easily get people to talk   ___ I work well alone

___ I need structure   ___ I can work with the handicapped

___ I can set up my own schedules

2. Look over the list and see if it includes all of the skills you think you have. If not, add any other skills you have acquired. The purpose is to get a sense of what you can do because that's a good clue to what your calling may be.

3. Now compare those skills to the activity that you imagine you might want to do as a life's calling. See how many match. List those. Then think about what skills you need to acquire to do your life's calling.

4. Take each skill you would have to develop and write about it in the following way:

* Describe the skill and indicate how you could get training for it, e.g., go to school for a degree, take one course, find a mentor, etc.

* Imagine doing what it would take to develop each skill on your list and describe how that would feel to you. If one of those means to an end seems uncomfortable or unfeasible to you— perhaps taking a community college course—try to imagine an alternative route, such as a course you can take at home on your computer. Then describe how that action feels. Keep doing this until you discover some means to develop a given skill that seems both practical and doable. If each avenue toward your goal feels uncomfortable, you may want to rethink your goal.

One other important thing to do when creating a safe space is to network into a group. I'm not talking about a psychological support group, but a group of people who knows what you're up to and will be there to encourage and assist you. They could also offer you opportunities to try out new skills and let you know of others who might be able to make connections for you. Whenever someone asks me what is the most important thing for a writer to do, I tell them to cultivate a friendship with someone who cares about their writing.

Another type of support is finding opportunities to volunteer at doing what you think you want to do. This lets you see how you actually like the job without the pressure of having to prove yourself. It also builds a networking group, as well as letting you know about paying opportunities that might be available in your field. A woman who wanted to be a social worker volunteered in a domestic violence shelter home. After working there without pay, she understood the job better and was able to get a recommendation to graduate school. She also stayed in touch with the staff to learn about what might be available when she graduated.

I started out writing for free for various small press outfits; I then moved up to working for a quarter of a penny per word. Doing that, I accumulated a short vita of publications, and eventually I was able to expect—and even demand—more for my work. Having some published works showed that I was willing to do whatever it took to get into this field.

★

Think back to the story I told earlier from *October Sky*. Recall how Homer Hickam envisioned a future for himself in rocket science, although he had poor math and science skills. As he set out to develop better skills (and to acquire some friends with those skills to help), he encountered many obstacles, particularly people close to him who began to chip away at his inner authority with their own worries and doubts. A boy like him could never be a rocket scientist, they said, and if he thinks so, there's something wrong with his way of thinking. When he succumbed to their authority rather than trusting his own, he lost his passion and surrendered to the dull routines of working in the mine. Yet something brought his vision back, and he decided to go for it, no matter what anyone said. He felt safer with that than with the plans that anyone else had for him. Fortunately, he was able to achieve not only self-trust, but the realization of his vision.

That is just how it should be for you. Once you feel safe with your own inner guidance, you can acquire skills and develop abilities to the point of melding your dream with reality. The following chapter takes you further into this area.

eight

INTUITION: TRUSTING YOUR INNER VOICE

★

People tend to distrust instinct, but intuition or the inner voice is the foundation of finding one's bliss. This chapter offers the touchstone of inner direction—intuition—and teaches you to develop and strengthen the ability to listen to your inner voice. Chapter nine presents more ways to strengthen your inner direction. Coordinating your emotional responses with your life circumstances helps you find the grand design of your purpose.

★ INTUITION ★

Intuition is often thought of as a sixth sense, or the way we utilize our inner awareness to provide self-guidance. Operating beyond our conscious awareness, it's a gut feeling on the border between cognitive and emotive skills that we act on in faith. Something inside tells us, without us having to slow down and analyze it, that what we're doing is correct. Those who regularly follow this sense of direction generally strengthen its power of insight. It becomes a sort of "knowing," an inner assurance.

Intuition can take many forms, the strongest of which

is the inner voice, which I discuss in detail below. Other forms include a feeling that something is going to happen, the sense that we must pay attention, any kind of fleeting clairvoyance or sudden energy, the feeling of peace, any seemingly significant encounter, a flow of inspiration, the easy visualization of steps in a plan, finishing someone else's thought, sensing a distant event that proves to have taken place and getting the flash of a name.

Intuition is about possibility. It often occurs serendipitously in the midst of some circumstance where it isn't necessarily expected. You might take a train trip and decide to change the seat you had originally picked. You don't know why, but you do it. Then you meet someone in the seat next to you who tells you something or connects you to someone that moves you forward. This is what happened to a young screenwriter who had recently moved into my area and was hoping to find other writers. She never talked with fellow passengers, she admitted, but something made her initiate a conversation with me. I offered her the name of a writers' network I was a member of, and that gave her some connections she needed.

Exercise

Take a few moments to think of something you need an answer to. Write down the problem, and then read over what you wrote. Meditate on it for a few minutes. Then browse through topics online, in a bookstore or in your own library. Something you see may produce an association that will present an answer. Many times intuition is simply a matter of letting ideas from within come to the surface by feeding them a little and coaxing them out.

It's also a good idea to write down on index cards fleeting ideas about the career that most interests you, save them in a box and, from time to time, look through them. You may find that your subconscious has made connections for you without your being aware of it and that some of these ideas fit together to give you a new inspiration or direction. You can use the same technique to develop a new direction within your career or to move you through an impasse.

You need to look at patterns, become mindfully aware of your daily activities, learn to trust your own subconscious direction and develop the ability to act on what you "know," regardless of the evidence or the majority opinion. What you have is a sense of vision radiating from the inner eye, similar to having a sense of rhythm from within.

In part, your ability to rely on intuition depends on your personal groundedness and sense of integrity. If you are honest with yourself and committed to knowing yourself, and if you seek balance and wholeness in all areas of your life, you are more apt to experience reliability in your intuitive skills than someone who is chaotic, dishonest and fragmented. Intuition works best when there's focus and the ability to allow the mind to yield its wisdom.

Most people tend to ignore these things or think of them as fleeting or coincidental, rather than paying attention in a way that will make them a significant part of their decision making. If you're serious about following your bliss, you need to start noting these moments and extending your awareness of them through practices (like meditation) that will quiet the rational mind and allow another form of "reasoning" to take place. The more value you place on intuition, the stronger your intuition will become.

★ The Inner Voice ★

To some people, it sounds suspicious to say that you have an inner voice. Nevertheless, guidance from within is welcomed by many people who lead otherwise normal lives. Often they won't talk about it because they have experienced the rebuff of those who simply won't accept the idea of subconscious guidance. However, many famous visionaries have counted on it to give them a sense of direction.

The inner voice is an auditory experience that seems to originate from within, not as a hallucination, but with the feeling that the voice is autonomous and, thus, unpredictable. Variously called the guardian spirit, the Master Mind, the white light, the Holy Spirit and intuition, it is often experienced as a sense of direction or enlightenment—even a warning. Psychiatrist M. Scott Peck talks about a client of his who was driving around a blind curve and felt the impulse to slow down substantially. "The thought suddenly occurred to me," he is quoted as saying, "that a car could be racing around the corner far into my side of the road." He braked just as a car came flying by, well over the line. Had he retained his initial speed, they would have collided. While he heard no words, the sense of an inner voice was evident in his experience.

The inner voice offers clarity, affirmation, advice and access to inner resources that you did not realize you had. Its vividness can vary from an inner impulse that has a verbal quality to actual language. The inner voice seems to manifest itself most often during times of crisis or the need for direction, although it's possible that this increase in messages may be due to your accessing your inner voice more often during these times.

"Stress and distress," says psychologist Stephen Martin, "weaken the ego's hold over the personality. At such times, inner states are activated."

It also comes during altered states of consciousness, such as relaxation, self-hypnosis or the blurred state just prior to falling asleep. Even more often, it uses dreams as a vehicle to get your attention or answer questions.

"I refer to the inner voice that so many of us hear during times of intense doubt," said psychologist Richard

Noll, "as the call of our inner personal daimon [guide]. I interpret it as the encouragement of our ancestors, a chorus speaking as one voice the ancient reassuring words of those generations whose genes we carry, that life *is* good and that it *is* worth all the confusion and pain that we may encounter."

Such voices are generally connected to personal circumstances, yet they seem to issue from an external source.

Verbal direction was fairly definite for Jackie, a professional in her midthirties who was going through a crisis. Putting aside some time to try to gain clarity from her suffering, each morning she went to a quiet place where she could focus without distraction on the pain in her body. There's no doubt this was a difficult exercise, but she felt that if she tried to avoid it by using numbing drugs or keeping busy, she would only put off the inevitable crisis. As she shed routine distractions, feeling the pain and waiting, her intuitive senses sharpened. "To my surprise," she remarked later, "I was confronted with hidden issues that had blocked my own growth. I thought I was just in a temporary crisis, but in fact, this could have been a long-term difficulty that I'd keep encountering."

As she acknowledged what she had learned and took steps to resolve some of it, the pain subsided and she managed to shift things in her life that would have taken her in a different direction. The daily lesson came to her in the form of words that formed for her, not as if someone was audibly speaking but as if sentences were floating up from the bottom of a still pond. With each step and each resolution, she gained further information. "It was like having a conversation with another part of me," she said, "a wiser, more centered part."

Inner voice phenomena span many cultures and areas. The ancient philosopher Socrates referred to his guiding light as his *daimon*. To him, it was a source of truth that directed his actions, particularly forbidding him from doing something that might endanger him. His most famous student, Plato, who wrote the Allegory of the Cave, also wrote that "the intuitions of the godlike are more valid than those of other men," and he urged seekers of wisdom to nurture that connection. Later, the Romans translated daimon as guardian spirit—"the one who can see to the bottom of uncertain situations and can give warning."

Christianity divided guardian spirits into devils and angels, the good guiding us toward compassion, generosity and holiness, and the bad toward narcissism, greed and violence. However, the early church discouraged personal visions and took over the authority of the inner voice. Anyone who came forward to say that she had received divine guidance, such as the children who saw the apparition of the Virgin Mary at Fatima, was subjected to rigorous examination, or worse. Joan of Arc was burned at the stake for declaring that she heard the voices of saints. Whether she did or did not is less the issue than the way the church at that time treated a personal connection with inner authority. This distrust has become a hallmark of our own culture. We tend to fear people who claim inner guidance rather than revere them or seek them out for life enhancement. We're suspicious of shamans and visionaries, and thus we fail to learn from them.

Alchemists, too, focused on sacred experience, engaging inner guides as teachers of secret wisdom. The *Lexicon of Alchemy* by Martinus Rulandus defined the practice as "the name of an Internal Talk of one person with another who is invisible, as in the invocation of the Deity, or communion with one's self, or with one's Good Angel."

Shamans have a long tradition of "otherworldy" guidance gained during trances or altered mental states. The Zuni Indians, for example, received their spiritual direction from fetish figures, while Persian mystics worked themselves into ecstatic states toward the goal of encountering figures of light usually glimpsed only in death. This experience, they claimed, was a way to experience within themselves the unity of the universe.

Exercise

Think of a person whom you might consider to be a visionary. Write down the reason you think so and what that person has done. Describe what it would feel like to be in that person's position. What would you do with such talent?

In modern times, the inner voice has been acknowledged by poets, authors, artists, musicians, healers, "channelers" and even ordinary folks. Mahatma Gandhi described a voice that advised him with the message: "You are on the right track; move neither to your left nor right, but keep to the straight and narrow." The words or ideas just come, these people report, as if writing themselves. Quite often they're surprised by what they receive.

However, the experience cannot be forced. It can only be nurtured and seduced with inner preparation, such as meditation that is developed as an internal dialogue of self-trust. If you are interested in developing your inner voice, attend to your flow of experience and listen to your thoughts without trying to direct or change them. Within those thoughts, you can often find important insights into your personal issues.

THE ORIGIN OF THE INNER VOICE

The question is, do these "voices" have independent existence or are they just a projection of an inner state from which we are so removed we don't even recognize ourselves?

One of the most influential contemporary leaders in the movement to trust our internal guidance was the Swiss psychiatrist Carl Jung, noted early in this century for his analysis of how other cultures express their collective beliefs. He also examined paranormal concepts and developed sufficient openness to unique experiences to develop access to an imaginal being whom he called Philemon. This entity came to him, he explained, as both a vision and an inner voice. "I observed clearly that it was Philemon who spoke, not I," he said.

His followers have explained this as one level of the psyche communicating with another level, rather than as some sort of spirit guide that attaches itself to us. Nevertheless, Jung saw Philemon as a figure who "represented a force which is not myself." He used a technique called active imagination—achieving dialogue with inner parts of the self—to engage Philemon in conversation. Philemon then made observations that startled Jung and transformed his theory of the unconscious realm. "I understood," he concluded, "that there is something in me which can say things I do not know and do not intend."

Dr. Martin explained it this way: "Jung would say that the voices are the expression of split-off parts of the personality that have psychological autonomy, as if they had a life of their own. So an individual experiences them as separate from his or her consciousness."

Jung did indeed believe that human consciousness is partly aware and partly unconscious, with the second part able to transcend space and time. Distinctions drawn by the conscious mind, such as "inner" and "outer," are not made by the unconscious mind, which helps us to feel what it is like to free ourselves of certain boundaries.

Jung conjectured that there is a part of us that is incomprehensible to our conscious mind. "The unconscious of man," he said, "can reach God knows where." That is, the conscious and unconscious minds are joined in a tension of opposites—one limited and the other unlimited—inside a union that we call self. The conscious mind is aware of our actual situation and the unconscious faces us toward possibility. Jung referred to this as "the future things that are taking shape in me" (In other words, our potential). Whether we cling to our limits or take steps to stretch them often depends on how much we trust our inner voice. In turn, how much we trust our inner voice will greatly influence how quickly we find our bliss and how willing we are to take the necessary steps to follow it.

★ The Balanced Self ★

The human psyche is attracted to the influence of wholeness. We actually desire to move toward all that we can be, although our conscious mind may fear going too far and thus hold us back. Nevertheless, our personalities are balanced only when these conflicting elements are integrated.

Thus, as we experience an increasingly clearer sense of inner direction, we become more truly ourselves. Accordingly, bliss connects with this idea. As Joseph Campbell indicated, it is "the thing that gets you deep in the gut and that you feel is your life." Learning to trust your inner voice will help you discover what it is you most want to do.

Unresolved inclinations lie dormant within us. As parts of a living psyche motivated by the force of balance, these inclinations are infused with psychic energy and eventually demand expression. The unconscious may then provoke involuntary phenomena like visions, dreams and voices, to move us along. Jung's Philemon and Socrates' daimon are among the most vivid examples on record.

"When someone is in close contact in a healthy way with their internal life," says Dr. Martin, "the voices can be illuminating and can have positive ramifications for psychological development."

To sum this up, the apparent autonomy of the inner voice, then, is the result of part of the self being separated from, and then possibly blocked by, an ego defending "the rational way." That makes it seem external. Nevertheless, the inner voice actually issues from within us and is part of our personal issues and desires.

Exercise

Think of a time when you felt guided by an inner voice. Describe it and relate it to either Philemon or the daimon. Add a few lines about how you decided to either trust it or not trust it, and indicate what you think that says about your potential to find your bliss.

NURTURING YOUR INNER VOICE

People for whom the boundary between the conscious and unconscious is not clearly established seem especially receptive to inner voices. That is, when the ego is consciously suspended, eroded by psychosomatic ailments or quieted through meditation, inner voices may emerge.

Some recipients welcome them and use them for growth. They integrate the voices, not just obey them. Whether inner voices are referred to as angels, spirit guides or internal dialogue seems to depend on the perspective, talent and beliefs of the person experiencing them. Utilizing the inner voice is not the only means of achieving greater psychological adaptation, but if it occurs, we ought to take note. "When you pay attention to inner figures," Dr. Martin points out, "they cohere. It means that the unconscious is telling you something extremely important."

Healthy people own the voices, discriminating good from bad to resist destructive or negative forces and acting on those that promise inner peace and well-being. They learn to integrate what they "hear" into their life situations in such a way that the voices are clearly functional. A man I know named Marty was a people-person, but he often went into job situations that failed to use his congeniality. One day he was offered a position as a salesman, but he hesitated to take it. Unsure of his ability in this area, he took time to give it some thought. An inner voice, he claimed, urged him toward it, so he carried on a sort of dialogue, writing down each part of his imagined conversation. In the end, he took the job, simply because that part of the dialogue seemed the strongest. Very quickly he felt that he had been born to it.

The ability to maximize the potential of the inner voice experience depends a lot on how receptive we are. According to those who nurture their inner voice and use it for direction, we must be open to whatever may be offered, even if it is contrary to what we want to hear. The inner voice does not necessarily support our personal agenda. It is there to draw us toward a form of self-achievement that is attuned to our sense of wholeness. We must also be willing to seek solitude, suspend judgment, believe in the experience and surrender to the state of consciousness that seems to defy rationality. That is, allow fantasy free play. We should attend to our intuitions, even if they seem out of kilter with our desires, let go of fear and utilize inner conflicts to break down our ego defenses and open up new channels of self-exploration and expression.

"The process is not of this world," insists Lee Coit in *Listening: How to Increase Awareness of Your Inner Guide*, "and therefore cannot really be explained in terms this world will easily accept."

Just remember a simple rule of thumb: Growth results in feelings of expansion, affirmation, direction and confidence, and the diminishment of fear and anger. Voices that encourage this ought also to be encouraged. Anything that conflicts ought to be released or avoided. To open yourself up is to transform yourself, so it must be done with care and discernment.

To further encourage the inner dialogue, I use two techniques: dream interpretation, including the development of an ability called lucid dreaming, and another that I've already mentioned—Jung's active imagination. In the next chapter, I'll explain these techniques and provide ways for you to utilize them. However, you first need to do some exercises in basic intuition. Each of these should be written in the section of your notebook devoted to this chapter.

Exercises

1. Describe a situation in which you made a choice under unclear conditions that you consider to be a mistake. Describe another situation in which you made a choice that turned out just right. Compare the two and decide how the right choice was made.

2. Select three experiences from your life in which you feel you acted in ways that turned out not to be in your best interest. Examine these experiences for patterns in how you made those choices, and make a list of steps you can take to correct your pattern.

3. Describe one instance in which you took a risk and it turned out much better than you expected. Describe how you made the decision to go ahead with that activity. Relate this to what you would do if given the choice to do something that once again seemed risky but also appeared to be the direction in which you wanted your life to go.

4. Write a paragraph about how your bliss would expand your life and make you more aware of your whole self.

nine

Developing Your Inner Guidance System

★

Intuition can take many forms, but two of the most productive seem to be the patterns of our dreams and the way we guide our imagination. By developing these aspects of ourselves, we can become more receptive to what our instincts are guiding us to do—we can hone our intuition so we can more easily find our bliss.

★ Using Dreams ★

A friend of mine whose talent involves entrepreneurial vision was getting lost in an increasingly frenetic lifestyle. She was late to meetings, misplaced important items and forgot some appointments. Even her home was becoming disorganized, which distressed her. One night she had a dream in which the two most important rooms in her home—where she would locate the seat of her soul—were going to be rebalanced with the Chinese system of *fen shui*. She knew little about this process, yet she realized that the dream was not directing her to hire a specialist in spiritual energy but to get her life into alignment with her spiritual direction. She began by organizing the clutter in her house so that the order of her personal space would reinforce the importance of extending the same balance to her career.

Sometimes bizarre and often perplexing dreams, like the one above, offer us many things: guidance, self-revelation, growth and even healing. They can assist with creativity, problem solving, stress reduction and life direction. Dreams can even help us become more proactive.

Award-winning set designer and children's book illustrator Maurice Sendak said that while dreams do not directly influence the content of his work, they raise the emotional level of whatever he is working on at that moment. He views them as part of the sequential order of the artist's subconscious life, and he does not question or resist them, but trusts them instinctively. If you are ambivalent about a project, a dream can help clarify how you really feel about it. Poet Maya Angelou has a recurring dream that signals when her work is going well. In her dream, she sees a tall building under construction, and she's climbing up inside it. (She declines to discuss dreams she has when the work is going badly because she believes that empowers the negativity.)

Not all dreams have that significant quality of heightening your awareness of some situation. They don't all have answers, nor are they necessarily symbolic of something you're struggling with. However, you can learn to pay attention to those that are helpful, and even train your mind to deliver a progression of dreams—resolving the issues brought forth in one dream will allow you to take them up in a more advanced state in the next night's dream. This has happened to me, and I've taught it in dream workshops, so I know it can work. However, two things are required:

1. Discipline to attend to dream recording and reflection each morning
2. Courage to face what you learn and to act on it

Those people who claim they don't dream, in fact, do. They may not think much about it when they awaken. Whatever brief images they might have remembered are gone so fast, it seems as if they didn't dream. Yet you can train yourself to recall dreams and to get increasingly better at it. The more you make this a discipline, the more you will be able to recall. It operates on the body memory principle: If you get used to getting up and writing down your dreams, your body will start delivering them with greater regularity and in more detail.

One way to start getting more than a glimpse of a dream is to set an alarm to wake yourself up at night. You may interrupt a rapid eye movement (REM) cycle, a period of sleep in which we dream more intensely. Another technique is to wake up about forty-five minutes before you normally do and then allow yourself a light doze. I've had some of my most vivid dreams during this state, with very good recall.

Once you start to get a glimpse of a dream image or memory fragment, write it down in as much detail as you can. Don't worry about whether it makes sense or has some deeper meaning. Do this every day so your body will soon learn the habit. After that, you can pay more attention to interpretation.

Tip: When you wake up, don't move from the position you're in. Stay that way and try to recall any dreams you had. Don't move until you remember as much detail as you can.

Exercise

Start keeping track of your dreams in your notebook. From this moment on, record everything you dream, especially in regard to the material you are thinking about. Whenever you have dreams that appear to be related to your bliss, write those down in as much detail as possible.

If you have trouble getting results, you can work with your daydreams or with active imagination, which is detailed below.

USING THE STUFF OF YOUR DREAMS

Once you have had some practice at recalling your dreams and writing the details, you can work dreams into an inner voice medium. For example, you might put a specific problem to your subconscious mind by meditating on it when you go to bed—stay focused!—and then asking your subconscious to provide a solution. It's often there in some dream image or situation. Even if you have no clear dream recall in the morning, it may pop up at some point during the day, such as during a daydream or as part of an association with something you and another person say to each other. Best-seller Sue Grafton uses this technique to solve problems with her writing. As she's drifting off to sleep, she suggests to herself that a solution will be there when she awakens, and more often than not, it is. She attributes this to her right brain processing the solution while her left brain is too deeply asleep to block it. To her, the right brain, like a dream, is whimsical and playful.

You can possibly make this work better for yourself by using some metaphoric imagery. Turn your question or problem into something that seems concrete, like bread dough that is placed in an oven or a sheaf of papers being placed in an "outgoing" file. Whatever it takes to get you viewing the problem as something to be processed or transformed in some way is what you should use. When you wake up, open the oven or look into the "in" file, and see what you find. It may not be what you expected, but don't reject any seemingly unrelated image. Upon reflection, you might be surprised by how relevant the image is to your "answer." The subconscious often works by association.

If you can, take time to allow the image or answer to

unfold in your mind. Take a walk, do some stream-of-consciousness writing or meditate. It might be helpful to explicitly ask your subconscious mind for a gift. It's there and may take more than one try to retrieve it depending on how open or disciplined you are. Or you may want to ask for a word or phrase, and whatever comes, be sure to write it down even (and especially) if you think it's irrelevant or confusing. You may soon have an "aha!" type experience.

To reinforce it, try doing this exercise several nights in a row. Write down what you get each morning without any kind of reflection or analysis. Then look at all of your entries and see if there is a pattern or progression. (I generally won't help people interpret dreams unless they bring me four that they have had in a relatively short period of time because I think dreams operate in patterns—especially emotional patterns—and you learn the most by seeing them in a context.)

Exercises

1. Try one or more of the techniques mentioned above, and write the results in your notebook.

2. Think about the following:

William Styron woke up one morning in 1974 to the lingering image of a woman he recalled from earlier in his life. He saw her clearly and knew that he must stop working on whatever he was doing and move directly into this image. This "woman" had a story and it became the powerful novel, *Sophie's Choice*.

Now sift through your own notebook or investigate your recurring daydreams, and find an image that sticks with you. Take the image (person, animal, object, place) and imagine a new scenario for it that will extend its power in your life. If possible, connect the image to any ideas you have about your life direction, and see how it speaks to you.

A lucid dream is the type of dream in which the dreamer becomes aware that he is dreaming. Generally, the dream is an exhilarating experience, especially when it becomes clear that the dream can be controlled by the dreamer. It becomes a sort of self-imposed trance. The dreamer does not wonder whether he is dreaming, but actually knows he is. These dreams can be either intellectually lucid or experientially lucid. In the former, the dreamer finds the content irresistible and may still experience reactions to it. In the latter, the dreamer is fully aware of his degree of control and exercises more options.

Surveys have found that as many as 50 percent of us have lucid dreams. Most lucid dreamers are good at visual tasks, are able to induce trances or to meditate, and have good balance. There are those who are so good at this technique that they can signal to dream researchers when they are having a lucid dream.

The most common occurrence of lucidity can be during a nightmare. The subconcious is presenting a context for resolving some disturbing or frightening situation. It is also presenting the dreamer with an exercise in getting it resolved: If the dreamer realizes that he or she has control, the dream material can take many different forms. Thus the dreamer can diffuse the emotional content of the situation. For example, someone with text anxiety who is facing an exam may dream about being caught inside a trap. The dream offers the opportunity for the dreamer to find a way out of the trap or even to dissolve the trap imagery. This kind of skill takes some work, but lucid dreaming can be a wonderful way to work out shadow material.

Lucid dreams end by the dreamer either waking up or losing the sense of lucidity. It is not uncommon, however, for lucid dreams to contain false awakenings: You believe you've woken up but you're actually still dreaming. In that case, if you realize it, you can continue to work with the imagery.

Lucid dreaming can be a valuable tool for seeking our bliss. It helps to reveal our blindspots and give us a sense of control. Self-awareness, along with the confidence that we are the captains of our fate, facilitates our forward momentum.

As a way to develop your potential to have lucid dreams, try the following exercise.

Exercise

Before going to sleep, concentrate on breathing evenly and deeply. Try to avoid being distracted with thoughts about your day or what you might do tomorrow. It may help to concentrate as you breath on relaxing the various parts of your body. Start with your toes. Tense them, and then relax. Do this three times, and then do the same with your feet, your calves and on up until you have relaxed your entire body. Keep breathing throughout. By the time you are done, you should be in a light trance, which means that you're feeling fluid and light. Then ask yourself, "Is this a dream?"

Do this several times. If you fall asleep and discover that you did not have a lucid dream that night (that you can recall), do the same exercise again the following night. Create an expectation that you *will* have a lucid dream. As part of that expectation, tell yourself that once you become aware that you are dreaming, you will actively work with the imagery.

Another exercise you can do before falling asleep is to tell yourself what you want to achieve in a dream. Use a meditative trance to repeat this to yourself.

Make sure you write down any and all results in your notebook.

Please note: There are no reported ill effects from taking control of your dreams. Cultivating lucid dreams makes for a more mindful waking state. It also helps you to feel more empowered when in challenging situations.

★ Active Imagination ★

Carl Jung describes his technique of active imagination in a work called "The Transcendent Function," written in 1916. When his break with Sigmund Freud brought him to the point of nervous collapse, he thought he might go mad. At first he resisted the feeling that he was losing his stability, but then he stopped being afraid. It was within that moment of surrender that he saw the possibility of making himself into a visionary on his own behalf: He could use his "madness," whatever it was, to teach him about his issues. Grim determination to not succumb when the mind is under stress often blocks its creative momentum, he discovered. When Jung decided to just let go, he found that he did *not* suffer the breakdown that he had feared, but in fact found a new freedom.

This freedom came in the form of what he called a "hidden ally." The subjective or inner mind was seeking expression against the restrictions of the rational mind. In the process of one struggling against the other, he used up mental energy that could have been directed more creatively. Jung surrendered to it and got what he called a "waking dream"—the lucid experience of a vision. Others have known this experience as well. In this same state, some people claim to feel light and animated, even that they are rising out of themselves and are able to go places without their body. The inner mind, when allowed, can show us the way out of an impasse that the rational mind cannot figure out.

After this experience, Jung felt he had achieved a better sense of balance between the conscious and unconscious mind, allowing his inner state fuller expression. It was an important step for him to break away from the ideas of someone else and develop his own. Had this not happened, Jung might not have discovered his true calling.

Active imagination, known simply as AI, is similar to lucid dreaming, but it does not take place while you are sleeping. It works more with the imagery of daydreams or fantasies that you develop through meditation.

The starting point is your emotional state. For our purposes, I'm talking about the confusion you may have about what you want to do in life, the frustration that you are not doing what you want or the feeling of being hampered by some set of circumstances. (The reason you are reading this book, I assume, is because you haven't arrived at your bliss, so there must be some negative emotional quality attached to that.)

The first step in AI is to be alone and free of distraction, as if you were going to meditate. Think of this process as tapping into an ongoing dream that usually surfaces only when you are asleep, but can be brought forth in an altered state as well. It's important to allow whatever comes forth to do so in its own way, but the real work comes when the image begins to sink back into your subconscious. You must stay focused. Once brought forth, you work with the image to extract its treasures.

Exercise

The initial steps involve the following procedure:

1. Make yourself as conscious as possible of the emotional state you experience when you imagine yourself following your bliss. Sink into it without reserve or self-judgment.

2. Jot down in your notebook whatever fantasies arise in this state, and any other associations that come up.

3. Allow your fantasy free play, but guide it to remain within the associated orbit, not simply to free-associate.

4. Remain relaxed but vigilant and attentive to the images that come. For now, make the list and keep it for reference later.

Yielding to the subconscious feels a little like falling backward into someone else's arms—there's a huge trust factor involved, but if you can do it, you achieve an altered state of awareness. "The whole procedure," said Jung, "is a kind of enrichment and clarification of the affect [feeling state], whereby the affect and its contents are brought nearer to consciousness."

At this point, you may actually hear an inner voice—an auditory hallucination, of sorts, as Jung had with Philemon. Primarily, however, you will get sensory impressions or images. You need to practice being aware of the images before you can do the next part. Make them three-dimensional and vivid. Practice holding one or two central images in your mind for as long as you can.

Now you're ready for the next step. You can do this alone, but you can achieve good results by doing it with a supervising friend or even a therapist experienced with this technique.

Exercise

1. Lie or sit still. Become fully relaxed, but remain alert.

2. Place yourself in a listening state, as if you know there is someone there who desires to communicate with you.

3. Instruct him or her—you can even call this imaginary person by name—to go ahead and say the message, but ask for the message in the form of an image.

4. Start with this image. (If you have a difficult time engaging an invisible person in conversation, select an image from your personal "cabinet" or from the list in the exercise you did above. It can be something from a dream, daydream or recurring image that comes when you're under stress. It should be an image that has some significance for you.)

5. Contemplate it. Carefully observe how it unfolds or changes. Record this in your notebook. Don't attempt to change it into anything. Just observe how it spontaneously unfolds.

6. Hold fast to the image. Let it change on its own but don't lose focus on that image. Turn it around in your mind until you know all the sides of it, and if it changes, allow it to change, but return to your original impression before proceeding.

7. Once you know the image well, step into the scenario. Speak to the image. Say whatever you feel is appropriate.

8. Allow the image to speak to you or to deliver a message in its own way. If it seems that a dialogue is forthcoming, go ahead and move into it. Once you feel you've gotten closure on the dialogue, go to the next step.

9. Ask the image for a gift. Don't allow it to fade, but give it time to yield to you what it offers. You've brought it forth from your own inner depths for a reason. Find out what it may give to you that you did not anticipate. Often, the message of some given image is not as obvious as it may seem. Tarry with the image until you feel it has fulfilled its purpose.

10. Be sure to write down everything you can recall about this experience because it may be useful to return to this image in a new way.

I once did this exercise in a group setting. We had been working with dreams, and it seemed to me the group was now ready for an exercise. I had each of them meditate on an image for awhile and privately describe it in writing. (It would be shared with the group later). Then I took them through the steps listed above.

One young woman, Sharon, described a disturbing dream she had had the previous week about violence, and the image she selected from the dream was a revolver. She allowed the revolver to rotate, seemingly suspended in the air in front of her, finally pointing its muzzle right at her. The image scared her, but she continued to allow it to be whatever it was in order to explore what her dream might have been about. On one level, she knew she was safe, even as she experienced fear (which was clearly the emotional content of the dream that included this image). When Sharon stepped into the scenario, she was able to touch the gun and then put her finger on the trigger. It yielded a feeling of power and she no longer felt so vulnerable. That was the gift—that what she was afraid of in her life could become a tool to allow her to live more fully. The dream was not so much about violence, as she had first believed, but about her own fears and the fact that she could not easily approach them and see within them her own resources.

Active imagination is not about the ego directing the subconscious to come up with rules to serve its limited agenda. Instead, it is intended for finding a way to be both receptive and directive—taking what comes in the dream and moving it onward. In this way, you can more directly flow with your movement toward wholeness, toward what your self wants and needs.

★ Combining AI and Dream Interpretation: Daydreams ★

Whenever you find yourself daydreaming in a way that has a recurring theme, symbol or character, practice the technique of active imagination as outlined in the steps above. If Jung's suspicion that you are always having a dream but are not always aware of it is right, then a daydream can be as fruitful as a nighttime dream. It's like lucid dreaming without going to sleep.

Exercise

Write down one of your most interesting or frequently recurring daydreams. Be as detailed as possible. Give yourself time to do this exercise because it is often difficult to recall the specifics of a daydream. Work with it as you did with the dream image above, and compare your results from the two exercises.

A side note: Dreams that disturb or frighten us often contain material that we need to work with more intensely. You might wish to consult a therapist to assist you in facing difficult images and themes, but don't avoid using this technique with those darker dreams. They, too, come from within you and have a message. If you ignore them in the hope of escaping the painful or frightening feelings, it is likely that you will continue to have disturbing dreams.

While I was separating from my husband, I had a series of dreams about myself. Since I was alone, they were even more frightening than they might have been had I had someone's support, but I was determined to find out what these dreams were telling me. As I stayed with the imagery of each one and gleaned some meaning from it, I received yet another dream that taught me something more advanced. This was a very dark time for me, and I wanted the dreams to stop, but when I refused to work with them, I just kept having more. Eventually, as I worked my way through them over the course of several months, I had an insight about a behavior I needed to change that was highly revealing. Once I took the steps to do so, the disturbing dreams diminished and were replaced by dreams of transcendence and great spiritual enhancement. I'd gladly go through another dark time to once again experience revelations of that magnitude.

★

The regular successful use of active imagination leads to a more synchronistic lifestyle, one in which you feel connected to the universe in a more mystical way. Things begin to happen when you need them to, such as someone giving you the answer to an important question or a door opening just when you need it to. And when you are open to inner possibility, you are open to finding your bliss. That brings us to the subject of the next chapter: synchronicity and its relationship to opportunity.

ten

BECOMING INTENTIONAL

✫

I was walking up Eighth Avenue in Manhattan when the lyrics of a song came to me, and I began to hum it as I walked. About half an hour later, as I entered a building, still vaguely humming this song, I heard it playing over the music system at exactly the point that I was at.

That's an amazing coincidence, and it's also the basis for the idea of synchronicity: We are so attuned to the deeper rhythms of nature and self that things seem to be magically coordinated. But synchronicity goes a step further. It's when events mesh in such a manner that they seem to magically work out in just the right way at just the time we need them. It's *meaningful* coincidence; it's not something we can predict or control, but we can learn to recognize and mine it for positive results.

Exercise

Make a list of recent coincidences you've experienced. Look at them for the possibility that these events coincided to make something work in your life. Hereafter, keep track of any other types of coincidences that happen to you, particularly on your bliss path. The more you notice them, the more you are able to follow in the direction they lead.

One of the most dramatic examples of synchronicity that I've heard was in a book on the subject by Alan Vaughan called *Incredible Coincidence*. (It not only affected me, but inspired the best-selling writer Dean Koontz to pen a novel about synchronicity.) It seems that a patrolman, Allan Falby, had crashed his motorcycle into the tailgate of a truck, rupturing an artery and nearly severing one of his legs. A businessman named Alfred Smith had witnessed the accident and used his tie to bind Falby's leg and save his life. Five years later, Falby was on highway night patrol when he was alerted to a nasty accident. He reached the wreck first and found that the victim was bleeding from a severed artery in his leg. Falby applied a tourniquet. Then he recognized the man as Smith, the same person who had saved *his* life.

In other words, one man saved the other, and thereby saved himself. What was more amazing is the mirror imagery of their respective injuries.

There's another amazing story about a man who came to Abraham Lincoln with a barrel full of books, looking for money. Wanting to help, Lincoln gave him one dollar for the lot. Among the contents of the barrel was a set of law books that Lincoln ended up reading. He went on to become a lawyer, and you know the rest of the story.

Such things happen a lot more than we realize, although we fail to attend to them because synchronicity is not usually so startling. It can be as simple as someone saying the right thing to make us think in a new direction. Our culture encourages us to dismiss the mystical qualities of such encounters, explaining such things away as "mere coincidence." Thus, we may fail to note things that are much more than "mere." When we're working toward growth and inner potential in terms of our bliss, we find that it is not just an individual process but part of a dynamic that affects society at large. If increasingly more people find their bliss, then more people will feel satisfied. It is also likely that those who find their bliss will contribute to the social well-being with their work. Additionally, as increasingly more people become attuned to the higher calling of bliss, the pool of those who can participate in synchonicity grows larger. They are doing what they are meant to do, so they may be in place to offer the right kind of advice or assistance to those still seeking. This has a positive snowball effect. Imagine a whole society of people who love what they do!

I was introduced to writing, which later became my profession, through a fairly amazing bit of synchronicity, which brought together seemingly unrelated events fourteen years apart. When I was seventeen years old, I had a boyfriend who asked to borrow some money, and I gave him all I had—two hundred dollars. He left town, and I didn't see him again. At this point, one might say I'd been conned (and it certainly appeared so to me at the time).

Fourteen years later, I was contemplating taking a writing course that cost two hundred dollars, and I didn't have the money for it. As the deadline approached, I was driving up the New Jersey Turnpike listening to the radio when I heard the voice of someone I knew: my former boyfriend. He was now a disc jockey and doing very well for himself—and he owed me two hundred dollars! I decided to contact him to see if he remembered. He did. Without hesitation, he paid me back. I used the money to enter the writing course, and by the end of the course, sold my first short story to an anthology that the instructor was putting together (and for which I was paid almost twice as much as the course had cost). That gave me the confidence to keep going, and fourteen books, numerous articles and several short stories later, I still recall how I got my start. When I tell that story, it seems to be just the right thing for other people to hear on their paths toward becoming a writer. Magic is contagious.

★ Deeper Into Synchronicity ★

Carl Jung introduced this concept in 1951, and it has become a major part of many New Age philosophies. Books such as *The Celestine Prophecy* by James Redfield present it as the basis for how people develop spiritually. Synchronicity is a principle that links events in a way that defies normal cause and effect. Instead, it fuels momentum. It connects the outer world with your inner psychic events. If you need to know something, the person with the right information will come along. If you are the one who is to be an agent in someone else's life, you will be inspired to encounter that person at the right time and in just the right way— though you may not realize how powerful that encounter will be for that person.

I've often been surprised by how someone reacts to something I've said that is insignificant to me but made all the difference in some impending decision to him or her. I was seated on a plane next to a young woman who was struggling with a decision about where to go to college. Since she had told me her top two choices, I was able to fill in the blanks for her and by the end of the flight, she knew what she was going to do.

This is not to say that the outward circumstance of an encounter is caused by the inner process or need. It is merely an indication of a larger connectedness between your personal world and the bigger picture. The feeling quality produced from the awareness that something significant—even transformative—has occurred exudes energy and a sense of rightness or direction. We feel part of a larger whole; we are "plugged in."

Yet it does not necessarily feel "right" all at once. That's what makes synchronicity so tricky. One woman told me the story of her cousin who had made it to Broadway. Initially, her cousin had been invited through an audition to do a part on a television show that she felt would give her little exposure and perhaps even hurt her credibility. It seemed a questionable step in her career, and yet it wasn't something she could easily turn down. A nagging feeling told her she should go ahead and do it, and hope that it wouldn't be damaging in the long run. So she accepted the part. To her astonishment, a major figure in the theater world was watching the show—something that he was not in the habit of doing. When he heard her powerful voice, he contacted the producers of the show and got information about her. Then he invited her to try for some parts on stage, which subsequently were offered to her, and soon she had a fairly secure singing gig and went on to get an award nomination. So it's not always clear whether one thing will lead to another. Just because some situation appears unlikely to lead anywhere, given the forces of synchronicity, you can never be sure.

Exercise

Think of a time you had to make a decision but didn't quite know what the consequences could be. That decision turned out better for you than you had imagined. Write down the circumstances, the nature of the decision and how you decided to go through with it. If you can remember, pay special attention to the role your body played. The singer in the example above had a nagging feeling that she should take the role. Is that part of your experience?

What you should begin to see is how your mind and body work together to guide you. It's not just about contemplating some potential direction, with all of its pros and cons. The idea of bliss is that there is something you are meant to do, and the forces of synchronicity work with that plan to provide mental and physical direction. You have to learn to pay attention to the signs.

★ It's Not All Magic ★

I might add that those who look for synchronicity under every rock can sometimes set themselves up to overinterpret any given event. They view synchronicity as magic and forget that there is personal work to be done to join one's preparation with those forces. I heard someone mention that he had gone to a writers conference with a manuscript all ready to hand over to someone. He walked into a room and there he saw an agent that he'd been hoping to meet. He immediately went over and handed her the manuscript. Later, he imbued this encounter with the mystical qualities of some higher force bringing them together. However, the agent didn't feel the same way. She looked at the first few pages of his manuscript, realized he had not taken the time to learn simple grammar and immediately returned it. He "read" that as a closed door that put him back on the right track for the right person.

To my mind, a writer's conference is full of agents and editors, and just because you share an elevator with one or wear the same blue dress as another, doesn't make it synchronicity. Actually, synchronicity is best interpreted in retrospect, as you look back along the road to some success and see how the pieces fell into place. To attempt to view an ongoing situation as somehow magical or mystical may set you off in the wrong direction. In my experience, it's better to accept that synchronicity occurs, but to pay more attention to your intuition.

When synchronicity *does* happen, prepare yourself to be at the apex of those forces. When they swing your way, be ready to move toward possibility. In particular, you'll have to be able to shut out the negative voices that may indicate your instincts are wrong.

Recognizing the possibility that some event is synchronous is a first step toward grabbing opportunity. (Reread that sentence: Recognizing *the possibility*, not deciding that it indeed *is* synchronicity.) A woman I met named Carla had worked hard to operate her own homeopathy business. She had a good instinct for treating people and found it utterly satisfying. However, her husband resented that she was succeeding and eventually this, among other things, 146 | 147 led to divorce proceedings.

She had to ask herself if she was going in the right direction when the person she had been closest to was in such opposition to her business. However, she knew she could also interpret the divorce as a freeing agent. What came next was more difficult to fathom. He sued her for half of her business. To buy him out meant bankruptcy. How, she wondered, could she accept this turn of events as part of the bliss scenario? It seemed that doors were closing, not opening, and quite definitively. However, her gut instinct told her to stick with it, despite how things seemed.

Just before they went to court, someone who knew her husband influenced him to give up his lawsuit. This person offered him another opportunity that would be hindered should he get entangled in a lawsuit. He opted to give up the lawsuit and signed the business over to Carla. Although she could not have foreseen this turn of events, it appears that the forces of bliss had fueled her determination so that when she got the business free and clear, she was ready.

If you believe in your bliss and your instinct tells you you're on the right path, then no matter how the path appears ahead, you need to trust that something will open up in the right way at the right time. The process of bliss, like any spiritual endeavor, is not necessarily easy or comprehensible at each stage, but when synchronicity appears to be sliding in, you must be prepared to act on it. It's better to act and find out later you wrongly perceived the coincidence than not to act and find out you failed to see its significance. Just take care to follow your gut rather than use the events themselves as guides. Bliss involves momentum, and you have to set into motion those things in your life that will keep the momentum going. Learn how to be prepared.

Exercise

Select one of the following exercises to write about.

1. Look at your list from the first exercise in this chapter and select what seemed to be the most synchronistic coincidence in your life. Write down how you felt at the time. If you told another person about it, try to recall that person's response. Looking back, do you believe you might have done something differently had you recognized the possible meaning of that event? Did your body give you any signals that you may have misread? Were there any that you read correctly?

2. If you're unsure whether you've ever experienced synchronicity, read through the above stories again and imagine yourself in a scenario where you believe some synchronistic event has taken place. How would you respond?

★ Recognizing "Rightness" ★

In order to better assess when an opportunity is a stepping-stone in the right direction, you need to get acquainted with your values and skills. I've already introduced this in previous chapters, but now I will get into it more specifically. To find your bliss, you must be able to read the relevant aspects of an experience, so once again, you need to return to your past.

Exercise

Think about something you enjoy doing. It can be an activity, such as horseback riding, gardening or attending a poetry reading, or it can be a significant one-time experience that stands out to you. In your notebook, write down a detailed account of this activity or experience. To facilitate your description, visualize yourself doing it and try to bring back the feelings you have or had while doing it. Reexperience the pleasure, and try to pin down which aspects of the activity gave rise to the most enjoyment—that is, explain why you would want to do it again.

Write down:

1. The most significant emotion you experienced.

2. Whether this activity was solitary or involved others.

3. How long the pleasure lasted while you were engaged in it.

4. Whether it was relaxing or stimulating.

5. Whether pursuing a repeat of the experience would be easy or difficult, convenient or inconvenient.

6. Reasons why you have or have not pursued a repetition of it.

7. If there is an obstacle to pursuing it, what that obstacle is and whether the obstacle is insurmountable.

8. What got you interested in doing the activity in the first place.

9. Whether there are stages of feeling during the course of the activity, and what those stages are.

10. What the ultimate payoff was of doing the activity.

Now do something similar with a negative experience—something you would not wish to repeat. Describe the experience and answer the following questions:

1. What was the dominant emotion you felt?

2. How did this feel in your body?

3. What about the experience made you want it to end?

4. Did it involve other people?

5. How would you recognize whether you were going toward a similar experience?

6. If you've knowingly repeated that experience, what circumstances might you change to avoid it again?

Once you have some idea of what goes into the kind

of experience you want to have (and want to avoid), why it engages you and whether it's something you would surmount obstacles to do again, you will have a better idea of how to evaluate opportunities that come your way. You will also be able to recognize when you're on a path you don't wish to take. Synchronicity will not necessarily move you exclusively toward experiences that you value, but it is unlikely that it will move you toward things you want to avoid. More likely, it will work with who you are and what you are likely to respond to.

Recently I was shown the work of a man, whom I will call Ron, who loved being a stonemason. It might take him an entire day to cut the stone for a five-foot walkway, but he became completely engrossed in it and hoped to continue doing this work the rest of his life. His father and grandfather had been in the masonry business as well, but initially Ron had gone into another business. He had what he described as a "cushy" job in the corporate world, but it failed to satisfy him. He'd done stonemasonry since he was fourteen and knew how much he loved it, so he gave up a job that felt "wrong" for him to return to one in which he could work out a vision. While the importance of money receded, satisfaction became more prominent, and the doors opened up in that direction. His customers saw how much he put into his work and appreciated the artistry. Through word of mouth, he had an increasingly larger customer base. Ron had returned to what he loved and found no end to the opportunities to make it work for him. He knew what felt right and what felt wrong, and he made the decision to build on what he knew was his life's direction.

★ EFFECTOR Vs. REACTOR ★

Once you understand synchronicity, grow familiar with what feels right to you and learn to recognize opportunity, it's important to develop a proactive attitude. In other words, you must take the initiative and begin to make decisions about what plans you need to put into place.

Taking initiative can be intimidating, yet people who do so claim to feel better about themselves, have more energy and have a positive outlook on the future. Conversely, people who wait for someone else to take the initiative so they can react or respond generally feel trapped and powerless, even exploited. It's important to know your own patterns so you can make the most of the process of bliss, which to some extent requires initiative and self-empowered momentum.

Exercises

1. Select five situations from the following list and write down what you might do.

A. You see a situation in the workplace or among a group of friends that causes unnecessary stress. You think you have a solution, so you . . .

B. It becomes clear that a significant person in your life is taking you for granted. You're out to dinner and he or she makes a joke with the waiter about what you're wearing. You . . .

C. You're with a group of friends and they start to make off-color jokes that display a prejudice that makes you uncomfortable. You . . .

D. An organization whose efforts you support is seeking volunteers. You have the time, so you . . .

E. You have an addiction that you know must be brought under control and possibly abolished. You . . .

F. You're asked to speak on behalf of a friend or organization in front of a group. Your first reaction is . . .

G. You see a friend stuck in a bad situation that will probably only get worse. You . . .

H. You have an opportunity to learn a skill that you know you'll need in order to follow your bliss. You are among eight people chosen to work in a group with a mentor. You board a train and realize that the mentor is seated in front of you. You have not yet met, but you know that you will soon be in a close learning relationship with this person. You . . .

I. You don't have the finances to take a course you need to become what you want to be. You . . .

J. You're at an impasse with a difficult boss who has wrongly accused you of doing something devious. You . . .

K. While at a restaurant with a group, everyone else eats much more than you and then expects to split the bill evenly. You feel this is unfair. You . . .

L. Jobs on a team project get delegated, but you find out that the person on whom your own job depends has done shoddy work. You . . .

2. Now look over what you wrote and pick out at least three distinct patterns of behavior that show up. Write them down. (If you see more than three, write them all down.)

3. Compare your patterns with the list below and make a check beside each characteristic that fits you.

_____ I have a difficult time seeing from someone else's perspective.

_____ I feel I have no control over a situation.

_____ I tend to accept other's ideas about me.

_____ I see myself in terms of genetics—I can't help how I am.

_____ I will compromise myself for the sake of a relationship.

_____ I wait until someone asks for my ideas before speaking up.

_____ I see if someone else can do a job that I'm asked to do.

_____ I know what I want, but tend to complain about my situation rather than take real action.

_____ I make plans but often fail to follow through.

_____ I tell my ideas to others in the hope that someone else will take the necessary action.

_____ I avoid situations in which my opinion might be solicited.

_____ I remain silent when I am or someone else is insulted.

_____ I go along with a group even if their decision makes me uncomfortable.

_____ I pretend for the sake of appearance that I am fine even when I'm not.

_____ I tend to defer to someone else's judgment.

_____ I blame others for my unhappiness or insecurity.

_____ I am driven more by feelings and circumstances than by willpower.

_____ I wait to see what others will do before making a decision.

_____ I have trouble believing I can actually achieve something.

_____ I feel I need help even on projects I can do myself.

If you marked five or more of these items, then you may have a problem being proactive. Go on to the next step.

4. Look at the list below and select five that reflect a situation in which you displayed this trait.

_____ I can stand apart from my own perspective and feel empathy with others.

_____ I feel that I can rise above my circumstances and overcome a problem.

_____ I can speak out in a group when I'm uncomfortable with its decision.

_____ I can imagine things being done differently and take the initiative to do so.

_____ I can discipline myself to make important changes.

_____ I validate my own choice when someone questions my judgment.

_____ I know when self-respect demands that I leave a situation.

_____ I act immediately when I see a problem that no one else sees.

_____ I know when I'm treated unfairly and can tell the responsible party.

_____ I believe in my ideas and freely offer them in appropriate situations.

Each of these situations is an example of the ability to be your own person and take charge. The more checks you made on this

list, the more proactive you are. What this says is that you respect
yourself and your integrity sufficiently to protect your values. If
you have never been in one of these situations, but believe you
have experienced something similar, place a check next to the one
that comes closest or add your situation to the list. Use this list
to affirm your confidence in your ability to do what you believe is
right.

★ Self-Motivation ★

The ability to act on opportunities that may lead you directly into your bliss involves some enterprise on your part.
Opportunities are there as part of what Joseph Cambell
and Aristotle viewed as the arranging of external events to
respond to your talents. If your calling is within you and
if that calling is part of a universal momentum, then your
personal development will correlate with genuine opportunities out there in the world. The idea is that when the
student is ready, the teacher will come, but the student
must then take advantage, and that means inner-driven
action. If you tend to react rather than act, to hold back
and wait, to blame others, to find excuses why not, or to
complain about something you can actually change, then
you need to work on this before moving on. If you are a
blissful person, you feel that you are on the right course
and motivate yourself to take full advantage of a situation.
You are on the edge of your seat, ready to get to work.
Bliss is more like a channel into which you move than being
pulled along on a sled by someone else.

Exercise

Read the following story and write a response to it from what you
know about yourself. If you were in this woman's shoes, how
would you do things, and what would be the result of your actions?

Roberta, a community service worker, had long been influenced by her dreams. Leaving her job and returning to school to focus on studying mythology and symbolism, she subscribed to a newsletter devoted to professionals who were studying dreams. In the third issue, she saw that they were seeking an editor. This seemed the perfect job for her—that she was following her true heart's desire—even though she had no prior experience in publishing, the position paid nothing and the subscriber base was very small. Undaunted, she took it on, turning the newsletter into a substantial journal and learning what she could about distribution. From there, she looked into finding potential magazine distributors. She then had to set about convincing them that her publication (now a journal) was worth carrying. It was not long before she managed to get it into major bookstores and within one year, her subscriber base increased by 200 percent. It went on to become an internationally distributed publication, as well as a job that supported her. Her own interests seemed to coincide with an awakening interest in dreams across the country, and that's what synchronicity is all about: getting the right combination of events and talents to make one person's bliss coincide with that of many others.

It is true that the attitudes that work best for making your bliss happen are entrepreneurial in nature. It means being self-directed, imaginative and ready to move when the time is right. When you find yourself in circumstances that seem to affirm the direction you want to take, you must seize the moment and figure out how to move into it.

The following chapter will give you a way to do this more effectively.

eleven

MENTAL AGILITY

*

Sharon had a problem. She had started a new business—
a cooking school. Knowing that her bliss involved food
handling, and thus far having gotten all the right signals
about her direction, she was suddenly faced with competition. Another cooking school opened not far away, and
they seemed to have more money to advertise and draw
participants. Her first impulse was to close up shop and
tell herself she had no business thinking in such gran-
diose terms. That was her pattern. Opening up the
school had been a major shift in her usual mode of
operation.

Instead of just reacting, however, she sat down and
thought through the situation. Having competition was
not necessarily a bad thing, she told herself, but that
alone failed to reassure her about her life's direction.
She still felt like giving up because her attempt to reframe the situation was abstract. It did not give her any
motivation.

She went over her values and mapped out how she
had gotten to the point of opening a business. It still felt
completely right to her, despite this setback.

Then she realized the problem: She could not get past viewing the existence of this other business as a setback. Therein lay the very thing that was filling her with doubt. What she needed to do, she realized, was take a different view of this new development. Was there any way she could not only avoid thinking of it as a setback, but actually see it as a positive factor in the development of her calling? It was difficult for her to think about it positively because without customers, she couldn't pursue this venture as a career. However, envisioning her competition as a potential boost rather than a threat made her view the other person in friendlier terms.

She contacted the owner of the other business, and together they worked out a way for each of them to specialize and thereby draw a wider customer base through joint ventures and referrals. Sharon got some advantage from her competitor's superior advertising, and she was able to contribute with her own strengths. The apparent hindrance, with a bit of mental flexibility, turned into a boon.

★ Mental Flexibility ★

The first step in developing mental flexibility is to be able to shift with life's disappointments and opportunities, which involves being able to see things from different perspectives. Freedom from rigid mindsets, for example, seeing competition only as a threat, allows you to develop resilience, which is imperative in shedding limitations and moving you toward the direction that best resonates for you. You need to be able to interpret any situation in more than one way, and then you can use this ability to motivate you to make plans toward a goal.

By way of showing you how to become more mentally flexible, let me take you on a trip through truth—or what passes for it when we become mentally lazy.

Have you ever felt certain you knew something only to discover that what you thought you knew was not what you perceived it to be? During the nineteenth century, spiritualists saw streaking points of light, which they believed were psychically magnified air molecules. They developed a whole philosophy around this phenomenon and drew disciples into a new religion based on it. However, there was nothing mystical about these lights. They are now regarded as an entopic effect, or the way light passes through the retinal layers of the eye. It's called Scheerer's Phenomenon and can result from circulation disturbances in the eye membrane. Not a very spiritual concept.

On a more mundane level, I've had the experience of seeing a friend in the distance and, being certain of my recognition of him, accelerating my pace to meet him, only to find I was mistaken. Had you asked me before I realized this, I'd have said, "Yes, it's him. I know it is." However, I was wrong.

Even more dramatic is the story of a young man who was part of an experiment on eyewitness accuracy. In a classic experiment, a law professor hired someone to run into his classroom, grab his briefcase and run out. Then he asked his class to describe the "thief." Almost half the class believed quite firmly that they could identify him, although they variously described his clothing as checked, solid, blue or red, and his hair as anything from black to light brown. They were shown a photo lineup in which the man's photo was not even present, and most of them picked someone. Many of them said that they were quite confident they were correct. Even after they were told they were wrong, one young man kept insisting that he knew the photo he had picked was the guy. No matter what anyone said, this was the guy!

Confidence in and the accuracy of our perceptions

have been shown in numerous studies to be poorly corre-lated. Just because we're sure does not mean we're right. In fact, sometimes being so certain is a stumbling block. Like the young man in law school, some of us simply will *not* allow ourselves to be wrong, even if we are.

Exercise

In your notebook, write an example of a time when you were convinced you knew something that you later found out was erro-neous. If you're doing this in a group, read your experiences to one another to get a more varied sense of how this occurs in our lives. Make this example as vivid as possible. It can serve as a reminder that "truth" is not always what you believe it to be.

It's common to be mistaken in what you think you know. There are many reasons for this:

1. Your senses deceive you. As a simple example, take a straight stick and place it in a clear glass that is half-filled with water. The stick that was straight now appears to be bent. If you remove it from the water, it is straight again. If you were to rely solely on what your senses told you and not on other modes of reasoning, you would be forced to say that the stick bends in the water and straightens out again when it hits the air.

Another experiment: Place three bowls or buckets of water in a row. One of them should be hot, one cold and one warm. Stick your right hand in the cold water and your left in the hot. Then put both into the warm water and make a decision, based on your senses, whether the water in that bowl is warm or cool. You would be forced to admit that it is both!

2. Your memories deceive you. Think of a situation (and you might want to write this one in your book) in which you felt that you made a fool of yourself. Then ask someone who was there to relate his or her version of the story.

Chances are good that there are some things you forgot. Or ask a sibling to describe a family event that you both attended and vividly recall, and note the differences. (I once asked my sisters to tell me which songs they recalled my father singing while we were growing up, and each of us came up with different ones. I didn't remember some that they claimed he sang all the time, and they felt the same about those that I so strongly recalled.)

3. *Imagination fills in the gaps, sometimes with a lot of detail.* I was looking over the negatives of some photos I had taken before getting them processed. One negative had what looked like a boogeyman of some kind smack in the middle, and that picture had been taken in a town famous for a movie about a murderous witch. The eyes were bizarre, the hands were huge and the figure wore some sort of cloak. However, the negative was not that clear, so I couldn't tell what or who it was. I didn't remember taking it. Because of that, I was a little spooked. Yet during the time that I had to wait for it to be processed, I came up with an explanation: I must have asked Rick, the friend who was on that trip with me, to pose. Yes, in fact, I did recall asking him to pose in front of a particular building. I'd nearly run out of film and thought it would be fun to get one of him in that town. I distinctly remembered having such a thought. The reason his hands looked so large, I assumed, was due to the negative. The same for his eyes. By the time I went to pick up the photo, I was convinced that this was a picture of Rick and I'd be laughing at my initial impression.

However, it turned out not to be a photo of Rick at all. It was a picture I'd taken of someone's rendition of the witch that was sitting on a porch, like a Halloween display. What struck me as odd was my distinct memory of asking Rick to pose for me. In fact, I had no picture of him, so he had not posed for me at all. Yet had you asked me before I'd gotten the picture, I'd have sworn

I'd taken a picture of Rick.

4. Information presented factually is often incomplete or interpreted to serve someone's agenda. Read two magazines with different political slants covering the same story and you'll see what gets included and what gets left out. You'll also see how words are used to convey a certain impression. I once read an "objective" account of the 1932 Lindbergh kidnapping trial and was convinced from the evidence that Richard Hauptmann must have been the culprit. Then I read a book citing the many problems in the handling of evidence and witnesses, and there was plenty of material there to cast reasonable doubt. So I went back to the first account and saw that it had been written in cooperation with the police agency that had had jurisdiction; no writer gets *carte blanche* when agreeing to an official cooperation with those who have something to lose if certain revelations are made. All of the evidence complications had been left out of the account.

I then read another book that showed how the author of the *other* book had overlooked or reinterpreted certain things to make his version appear to be more reliable. In the end, I didn't know whom to believe.

There is also the problem with information presented in an ambiguous way so that the interpretation is left open or facts are cited that could not possibly be known. I once heard someone in authority claim that 30 percent of all date-rape cases go unreported. However, if they weren't reported, there is no way to know how many there are. I heard similar statistics about "unreported" workplace harassment from a woman claiming to stick closely to scientific methods.

It takes a fairly analytic mind to remain alert to the problems that occur when processing information into knowledge. Many people who have only speculative information want to present it as fact, and we need to be guarded in our appraisal. There is a great deal of sloppy reporting and since few of us take the time to check out sources or statistics, bad information comes our way in abundance.

★

Much of what we use in our day-to-day assessments is based on the appearance of things. We often depend on knowing by appearance, and some people have gone so far as to say that appearance is reality. Sometimes we have to make quick decisions based only on appearance: the fin slicing through water looks like a shark, so we'd better get out of the water, even if it's not.

The problem is that we come to rely on our judgment of appearances, and then become prone to being deceived. We know that the stick in the glass of water is not really bent, but not all illusions are so quickly detected, especially when others are acting on those appearances as if they *know*. Safety in numbers can become "truth," but this is a symptom of mental rigidity. We mindlessly follow rather than carefully reflect. Once we admit that appearances can be ambiguous, we are prepared to shift away from what is regarded as "truth" or the "only way to do it" and to move toward the possibility of options.

Exercises

To give yourself a quick lesson in mental flexibility, do the following puzzles:

1. Pick up a fork and write down what you do with it. Then write down five more things you could do with it that have nothing to do with a fork's typical function.

2. Imagine yourself as a travel agent with a radio show. You need to fill it with two guests each week. Once you have found everyone you can who is associated with the travel industry, think of imaginative ways to tie other topics to travel. List six.

3. Look over your workspace, no matter where it is, and redesign it in a way that would make you more effective. Then try yet another design for the same purpose.

4. Draw five rows of trees with four in each row to get only ten trees.

5. Use only four straight lines to connect all of these dots:

• • •

• • •

• • •

6. Now solve the following problem:

Harry is in a prison with concrete walls that extend several feet into the ground. The doors are impenetrable and the floor is made of packed earth. Eight feet overhead is a skylight, but there is nothing in the room upon which to climb. Harry is only six feet tall—too short to reach the skylight. Yet he escaped by digging a hole down into the floor and going out through the skylight. How is that possible?

(You'll find the answers to 4, 5 and 6 at the end of the chapter.)

★ BEYOND FLEXIBILITY ★

Mental flexibility is the skill of thinking beyond what we have been trained to do, defying traditional thinking and coming up with unique perspectives. *Mental agility* is being able to offer perspectives that include a plan of action. You apply mental flexibility to actual situations, coming up with several options to achieve a result.

Recall the previous tale from *The Little Prince*. A pilot is stuck in the desert and a little man comes along and urges him to set out into the arid wastes to find water. Now I have another, more creative exercise for you to write about.

Exercise

This is best done as a group exercise, but if you don't have a group, perhaps you can enlist a friend to give it a try.

Put yourself in the position of the pilot from that story. You have a defunct plane. Thus far, your tinkering has failed to produce positive results. You face the prospect of dying of thirst in the desert. Then you encounter a little man who claims to be a prince from another planet, and he offers a solution to your dilemma. Go walk into the desert.

Describe how you might react.

After you have finished, compare what you wrote with what someone else had to say. The more responses you see, the better.

Now write down what you learned about yourself when you compared your answer with what others had to say.

By all appearances, this little man was just a deluded midget, but if that's as far as you got, you have a lot of work to do to develop mental agility. This ability requires a certain amount of creativity, or working past—and outside of—artificial boundaries that are usually imposed by culture.

The way the story goes, the pilot finally decided to go with the prince, but before he did, he had to go through an exercise of mental agility—seemingly as a sort of test. This is what happened:

The prince asked the pilot to draw a sheep. He had need of a sheep, he explained, to eat the destructive "baobabs" on his planet, so his beloved rose could bloom. The pilot drew a basic picture, but the prince rejected it. The pilot tried again, and again failed to give the prince what he seemed to need. Finally, the pilot just drew a box with three tiny breathing holes and told the prince that the sheep was inside the box. The prince peered at the picture. Then he said he could see the sheep and it had gone to sleep. It was the pilot's first lesson in going beyond the superficial and envisioning possibilities that one might not think of right away.

Then he was ready, and although he was afraid that going into the desert meant certain death, they did, in the end, find water.

Whenever you prejudge a situation or cling to habit, you blind yourself to other possibilities. Mental agility requires flexibility followed by a creative approach and a course of action. First you need to realize that almost any situation can be viewed in more than one way, and second, you need to think of some of those ways.

Now it's time to apply these skills to your own situation. You have clarified your values, thought of how the "right" path feels, imagined what you think your bliss might be and looked at some of the ways you could block it. You've also given some thought to intuitive guidance. Regardless of whether or not you are right about the specific nature of your calling at this point, complete the following exercise as if you know what your bliss is.

Exercise

Do you want to pursue photography, cooking, computer repair, desktop publishing? Write down what it would mean to follow your bliss. Make a list of what stands in your way. Pick one item from that list and exercise some mental agility in finding your way around it.

★ USING FLEXIBILITY WITH VISUALIZATION ★

Once you have a good feel for how to be flexible with your perspective on a given situation, you can develop a tool that can help you to imagine diverse directions and outcomes.

Rachel wanted to start her own fitness business, but because she had children, she wanted it to be close to her home. When she went to look at potential rental spaces, she was disappointed with what she found. Nothing seemed quite right for what she had in mind. Yet she didn't want to go farther away. Her only option, aside from giving up, was to work with the spaces that were available. She went to the top three and visualized what they *could* be, given some work, and then imagined herself giving fitness classes there. As she did this exercise, she was able to eliminate those spaces that clearly could not be molded toward her purpose and to pick the one that appeared most adaptable.

Once she made that decision, she worked at visualizing her business starting in this space and growing. Some people use the term "manifesting" for this exercise; it's the idea that thinking about something in sufficient detail can make it happen. For Rachel, it served the purpose of clarifying her vision and keeping her motivated. She rehearsed the images to the point where she sincerely believed they would come about, and when she began to work to convert the rental space into an exercise studio, it seemed destined.

"When you imagine doing something in a certain way," say psychologists Bernie Zilbergeld and Arnold Lazarus, "the mind tends to take this as a real experience." Studies on the use of visualization in sports indicate that the respiratory and nervous systems respond as strongly to the mental experience of a sports event as to the actual physical experience. The mind is obviously quite powerful. It makes sense, then, that practiced imagery helps you become more engaged with the direction you want to take. You can use it, coupled with mental flexibility, to think of yourself along several potential paths so you can make better choices. You can visualize yourself toward your bliss.

Mentally putting yourself into a situation involves imagining many details, including noises, smells and bodily sensations associated with the situation. You need to make it as real as possible to build a body memory. The more vivid your imagination, the more effective the visualization will be. A report from the National Research Council in 1988 indicated that mental rehearsal had a significant impact on learning performance, so it's bound to do the same for your goals.

Use imagery and visualization to control how you think and feel about a situation, so you can avoid negative feelings like anger and frustration and move toward joy and fulfillment. There are two basic steps involved:

1. Relax. You need to make yourself comfortable to be able to fully take advantage of this method.

2. Stay focused. The image will recede unless you work hard to keep it in place.

Exercise

Find a distraction-free environment where you can relax and pay attention to your mental processes. Sit or lean back in a comfortable position, but don't become so comfortable that you are in danger of falling asleep. Bring to mind a situation you wish to envision, whether it is part of your path to bliss or something else like solving a problem or approaching a person you want to meet. Breathe deeply several times, clearing your mind of all distractions. Then imagine yourself in the situation, drawing on every relevant detail of the senses.

Watch yourself perform. What are you wearing? What do you see? Whom do you encounter? What do you do? What happens as a result of what you do? For now, just concentrate on all of the elements as you work your way through what you hope to accomplish.

Stay focused as you tighten and relax various muscles in your body, starting with your toes and working your way up to your face. Stay attuned to this imagery until you've moved through the entire scenario. Then get your notebook and write down what you recall.

Now you have a basis for practicing both mental flexibility and mental rehearsal. If you don't like some aspect of what happened, use flexibility to change it and work your way through other possibilities. Once you have the scenario set the way you want it, as Rachel did with her fitness center, keep going over it. Rehearsal sets it in your mind and gives you a sense of moving toward the future. Don't forget to write about it. If you can make a specific application to your life direction at this time, by all means do so.

What you may already realize is that visualization is a form of self-hypnosis and even a bit of active imagination. You control the content and intensity of your images and change them whenever you want. Anyone can achieve this, although it comes more quickly for some than for others. If you're having trouble, use past successes to help you to envision something similar in the future. For example, maybe you learned how to play a sport to the point of mastery. Recall how you did that and apply the same principles to what you hope to do in the future. You're like an actor getting ready for a part. You have to see yourself in it to do it well.

You can use visualization in so many ways, any of which can be helpful in the process of finding your bliss. You can use visualization to:

* Solve a problem
* Set a goal and see yourself achieving it
* Reduce the level of anxiety attached to a certain situation
* Raise your energy levels
* Improve your current performance
* Motivate yourself
* Master a skill
* Enhance the quality of your experience
* Try out different options
* Imagine the outcomes of your decisions

Now use some flexibility to think of more ways to use visualization. Even better, I'm sure you can practice more. In any event, these skills will assist you to become more fully actualized. The better you get at using them, the more creative you will be and the more likely to become focused and immersed in your bliss.

Answers to puzzles:

4. (Four in each row, five rows, ten trees)

5. (You have to draw outside the apparent frame.)

6. Harry dug a hole in order to pile up dirt until he was able to reach the skylight. To "get" this, you must first liberate your mind from the image suggested by digging *down.*

twelve

The Discipline of Bliss

★

Recently one morning, a friend of mine, Mike, called to say how much difficulty he was having with the idea of turning a large body of data into a book. He believed in himself as a writer, but something was missing in this particular project. Although he knew his bliss, he felt he had briefly gone off track.

"I can put one sentence after another," he moaned, "one paragraph after another, one chapter after another, but I still won't have a book. It's not just about information, or even about presenting it. There's something else. Do you know what I mean?"

I did indeed. Colin Wilson called it "Faculty X." By that he meant the ability to relax your mind enough to dissociate and move yourself into an altered mental state. In this state, you can almost experience another reality altogether, even visualize another time and place as if you were actually there. For example, Wilson was once daydreaming and the image of a spaceship came into his mind. He let it take shape and then mentally explored it for details (just like active imagination). Soon he had the sketch of a plot that became his third science fiction novel, *The Space*

Vampires, which was then turned into a film called *Life Force*. He used a state of relaxation to find a spiritual center. As Mike said above, it's not about putting one sentence after another. It's about finding a sense of how it all fits into a whole.

This applies not only to individual projects that are part of your bliss, but to the achievement of bliss itself. There is a spiritual center both within a project and within your life direction, and you need to locate it and keep yourself in touch with it.

Colin Wilson believes that this talent of allowing inspiration to unfold in a holistic manner can be trained toward greater creativity, so that anyone can become more like Mozart, who described music as "walking in his head." Wilson relates Faculty X to the theory that you have something like two selves within you—a creative self and an analytical self. These two parts process information at different speeds, and when you can set up conditions that coordinate them, you achieve maximum creativity. For example, you can soothe yourself into a state of deep relaxation or work yourself into a state of great excitation. Either way, you're trying to get the two selves to match more closely in their rate of processing. That puts you into a state of consciousness you don't fully understand, but also gives you access to abilities that otherwise lie dormant. When you achieve this balance, whatever you're writing (or otherwise doing in a blissful way) will seem to write itself.

I think the X-factor comes from deep immersion in your subject. People talk about "flow" as the union between you and your work, and I think that experience depends on how easily you can surrender, not just to the process, but also to the material. It's about trusting that the material has its own center and will show that center to you when you're ready to honor it. The same goes for bliss. You have to trust how the events are coordinated so that you can relax and move into the flow of it. Getting good at this with a specific project will develop your ability to do it on a larger scale.

In my own experience writing books—including this one—I start out with a nice idea about organization and development, but somehow it never works out according to my plan. I find myself wading into the material with the feeling that I'm floating in deep water. There's no land in sight, no boat, no rescue. I don't know where I'm going or whether anything will come of what I'm doing, but I'm groping toward the *key*, the heart of the book that will radiate out across the entire body of ideas and give them a narrative drive.

There have been times when I didn't find it and had to abandon the project. Like Mike said, having a large body of data, all nicely arranged, doesn't make a book. There's no spirit in it.

Since writing is my bliss, let me explain how that fits into the larger picture. Just as I immerse myself in an individual project with faith that it will all come together, so I follow my life direction with the same trust. Bliss is a spiritual venture that involves a sense of direction that fits *me*. Even when I don't always see where it's going, I trust that it will work out. The same goes for each project that appears to be part of my bliss. You "feel" your way through, even as you're thinking your way through.

Let me explain this further with a detailed example. Writing the life story of another person, as I did with Anne Rice and Dean Koontz, involves many levels of immersion. What you're hoping to grasp through all those layers is the secret—the momentum or the quick of that person's life; what motivates that person's character and subsequent future actions.

So you start with the basic facts: when and where they were born; what kind of family they grew up in; where they went to school; how they did in school; whether they had friends and what kinds of friends; how they first began to write; who inspired them; when they had their first success, their breakout success, their first hurdle, etc. Soon you find yourself overwhelmed by material, and you want to just start writing, to get it going so you don't drown in data. However, it's better to quell that urge and allow the material to settle in. Let the full abundance of material work on you for awhile. You immerse yourself so that you can think like them and even see things through their eyes.

For instance, rather than just mention that Anne Rice used to walk up St. Charles Avenue to school or through the Garden District of New Orleans, I went there and put myself in the mindset of a young girl walking from a small house past all these mansions and gardens. I *felt* what it would have been like for her, and by doing so, understood why she loved to go walking by herself, imagining stories taking place inside those houses.

I made a lot of notes so I wouldn't forget anything, but I primarily waited until I felt I had some core out of which everything else would grow. I spent a lot of time walking and processing the material without interpretation. I made a point of focusing on it before I went to sleep and recalling my dreams in the morning, searching for clues. Eventually the "aha!" happened and I was ready to roll. The life story fell into place with a nice rhythm that made the writing itself rewarding, as it ought to be, rather than feeling like a rock I'm endlessly rolling up a hill. I had a book because I knew the spirit from which it took form.

The same thing can happen in fiction. Many of my friends who write fiction describe how important it is to get to know their characters fully and to have all kinds of background on them that may never be mentioned. To create three-dimensional "people," they have to immerse themselves into those characters and see the world through their eyes.

Similarly, your own bliss-related project similarly will require your full commitment. The project, as it becomes part of the unfolding of bliss, will have a center that supports and flows from the bliss center. Trusting one involves trusting the other. The more complicated a project, the more difficult it may be to trust that the center is there, but if it is indeed part of your bliss, it will eventually become obvious how it fits into the overall plan. My biography of Rice, for example, led to more books with her and then to another biography. I could not foresee this from within any given project, but each was building toward the other. As I honed my ability to trust the project, I developed greater trust in the forces of bliss.

Exercise

Do one of the following:

1. Think of an activity in which you have immersed yourself in order to develop a skill or body of knowledge. Describe what that was like for you.

2. Create a character for a story and describe what you will need to do to really get to know that character.

3. Write about how you think that getting fully involved with a project is relevant to a better sense of your spiritual direction.

★ THE PSYCHOLOGY OF IMMERSION ★

Getting fully engaged with something is about crossing boundaries and merging into other worlds. It is an exercise in perception and in the ability to move more deeply into a sustained concentration. Finding your bliss, as I mentioned in the chapter on flow, will pay off in a heightened engagement with life—and in greater skill.

I once did an experiment with a class that was studying

literature. I told students that I would not be giving them grades along the way because I wanted them to attend to the material, not the external evaluation. In other words, I wanted to get them more deeply involved. At first they were annoyed, meaning they were probably afraid. They were used to a certain structure and knew what to expect from it. This was a new way of doing things.

Nevertheless, once they got used to the idea, they did get more involved in the class and soon forgot about the typical academic structure. Their discussions got better and it was clear they were focusing on the material and its relevance to their lives rather than on grades. They even turned in papers that showed they were more engaged with the subject than they ordinarily might have been. Each day they were confronted with wondering whether they were really learning something, which meant they were more likely to take active measures to move toward the material. They became fully absorbed—and it showed. When they were finally evaluated on the material in a mock exam format, they responded to it with a deeper knowledge than what they would have had they learned it by merely memorizing notes. Being immersed, they moved beyond mental into spiritual dimensions of their learning experience.

Immersion is going beyond ordinary levels of awareness. It is moving to a deepening engagement with a form of consciousness that comes with focused concentration. Those who achieve this can seem almost otherwordly.

Eugen Herrigel describes a time when he was in a meeting at a hotel in Japan. An earthquake occurred and the building began to sway. Most of the people at the meeting rushed out into the halls to try to escape, but Herrigel noticed one man still seated in the conference room. This man was completely calm, his hands folded, his eyes closed. The earthquake lasted for some time, and when it was over, everyone returned to the room. The Japanese man picked up the conversation precisely where he had left off, as if the recent event had failed to register at all. To Herrigel, it was an example of the most refined type of unassailable concentration. Zen practitioners work very hard to achieve this ability, but it's more available to all of us than most people realize.

This idea of sitting with such a focused mind is a meditative discipline. Your thinking is quieted, and you attempt to harmonize feelingly with the world. It is my experience that the more developed your concentration, the more likely it is that you will not only achieve bliss, but also get the most benefit from its spiritual qualities.

★ Forms of Consciousness ★

Most of our everyday encounters involve a sort of diffuse awareness of things that we're walking by, sitting on or using in some task. That's where we "live," so to speak, without giving it much thought. Psychologist Stephen Wolinksy calls this everyday existence a trance state; it's filled with personal concerns that blunt our senses and preoccupy us. We miss the best qualities of the moment.

The focused mind must be receptive, but not passive. It is free of mental hindrances like fear or self-criticism. We need to ready the mind for stillness.

Annie Dillard, in her acclaimed book, *Pilgrim at Tinker Creek*, shows what it means to adopt an attitude of quiet, attentive receptivity. She describes walking through the woods for long stretches and sitting around observing the intricate manifestations of nature. She doesn't decide what she wants to see, like going into a clothing store with a specific type of blouse in mind, but simply relaxes and stays alert to the phenomena. That way she doesn't miss something by focusing on what she thinks she wants to see. She allows nature to spontaneously appear as it is, even if nothing at all happens on any given day. As a result, she witnesses remarkable events among insects, wildlife and plant life that most people miss.

To become receptive, it's important to free our minds of mental noise and to learn to be aware of the present moment. Yes, we all have concerns and we're all bound to the past in many ways, but the present moment is where the most crystallized form of perception occurs. We need to practice letting go of distractions. This will help us become attuned to those intuitions that will assist us in finding and following our bliss.

There is power in the deeply hidden self, and if we stay at a surface awareness, we will miss the opportunity to tap and develop that power. Our learning will be superficial, our concentration fleeting and our souls will go hungry. Solitude, coupled with the ability to focus in a receptive way, can help draw out mental clarity and spontaneous creativity.

We can reap the benefits of a world teeming with activity only if we unburden ourselves and develop patience. We need to pause for a few moments on a regular basis to develop the art of receptivity.

Exercises

1. Set up a timer and allow yourself three full minutes to do nothing but be aware of what is in your surroundings. Do this for three days. Then increase the time to five minutes and repeat for three more days. Then increase the time to ten minutes. Make this a daily habit to allow yourself ten full minutes of being aware of yourself in the present. Write about what happened.

2. Go for a walk with a child and listen to how he or she pays attention to the world. Children are curious and intense, unencumbered by worries and biases. They take it all in. You may learn the ways of a quiet, awed simplicity. Write about your experience.

3. Take a walk in the woods like Annie Dillard did and allow yourself to notice what's there. Describe something about your experience that indicates a fresh perspective.

⋆ A Word About Trust ⋆

We're often encouraged to try hard to concentrate and as a result, we view it as work that we have to think about doing rather than as an experience we can slide into. Rather than *trying* to concentrate, it's more important to simply concentrate on something we want to do and allow the process to unfold.

Exercise

Try an experiment. Fill a bucket or bowl with water, nearly to the brim. Carry it across a yard and concentrate on it by looking directly at it, telling yourself not to spill any of it. Write about what happened and how you felt once you got all the way across.

Now do the same thing, but this time carry it without looking. Just trust your body and mind to work together. Write about what happened and how it felt. Were there any differences?

What does this tell you about trusting your inner direction?

In general, when we concentrate on concentration, we exhaust ourselves. Often it just doesn't work. Most people who try the above experiment spill more water when they look at what they are doing than when they trust their body to follow their mind's direction in a natural balance. Often, when you let go and trust this rhythm, you can do things you had not even imagined. You may have to relax some mental habits, but trust is an essential ingredient in mental agility as well as in the process of flow. It is also a key ingredient in finding your bliss. If you allow it rather than force it, your mind can be an automatic doer. Direction can come from within.

There are three levels of awareness that eventually merge into the kind of concentration that allows us to become immersed—or to sit through an earthquake. The third level is the one that will benefit you the most as you attempt to determine what you were born to do.

THE FIRST LEVEL OF AWARENESS

The first level of awareness—day-to-day consciousness—provides the foundation from which you move into other levels. It consists of a vague awareness of things in the external world, along with basic but undefined focus on those things that you need to pay attention to. Routine consciousness is generally mindless, moving in and out of focus in a fairly automatic manner. You may not even realize it's happening. As you drive, for example, you notice and respond to street signs and other cars, but at the end of the trip you probably could not list all of those instances. To get an idea of what I mean, just sit quietly for a moment in the way you ordinarily would. After a minute, pick something to focus on—a chair, vase or framed photograph. See how everything else recedes, allowing you to see that item more prominently? Now refocus on just the backdrop to that item and notice how the item itself becomes diffuse as you adjust your visual perception. This same phenomenon happens with the other senses as well. Focusing helps you get a defined perception of something. Not focusing gives you only a blur of items. We need the background in order to see a figure. We may not recall the figures we see as clearly as this experiment indicates because the process is generally part of our routines.

THE SECOND LEVEL OF AWARENESS

The second level of awareness involves paying closer attention to how we make a figure stand apart from background.

We tend to move into this second level when something requires our attention. For example, we concentrate on one building on a city block only when we have business there. We might also be pulled into the second level of awareness when startled, such as hearing a car run into something.

Rather then being reactive, your goal is to become more intentional about moving into the second level. You probably tend to notice something and then go back on "automatic pilot," pushing it into the background. As you develop a defined awareness, however, you notice more things. You become more attuned to the immediate world and develop a sharper sense of perception. Think of it as seeing a friend in a crowd of people. That person stands out because of what he or she means to you. Active perception means you grow more alert to *looking* for a friend in a crowd.

What turns one thing rather than another from background into figure is the attention you pay to it—the significance you attribute to it. That comes from your values, desires and needs. You wrap it in an emotional coating such as delight, attraction or discomfort.

This second level involves varying degrees of attention on a continuum from passive to mildly attentive to full consciousness. You are more engaged than at the first level, although you may only derive short-term benefits. It can merely become part of your routine, offering only superficial knowledge. That's why it's important to make the process of paying attention an end in itself, to derive the most from it. Bring it out and use it.

Exercise

Think of something from your life that illustrates the difference between the first and second levels of awareness. For example, recall a situation that demanded your attention, such as having to look for an address that is on a route that you normally travel without paying much attention. Make a note of things you notice now in this second level of awareness that you had not noticed before, although you passed it regularly. Try to determine how long you focus on something when engaged in the second level. Now make it a daily practice to pick something to focus on and extend the length of time you pay attention to it until you develop a more sustained practice of intentional focus. Describe what it is like and list three of the benefits.

THE THIRD LEVEL OF AWARENESS

Mastering the advantages of intentional focusing at the second level can lead to a deepening and active engagement—the third level of awareness. This is a more profound state of concentration that involves being mindfully engaged and alert to detail. It's about more than just locating an address or noticing the source of a loud noise. You are paying close attention to something, learning about it or becoming involved with it.

Everyone has had the experience of what I call a "quickening"—a resonance with some subject they want to know more about. I once interviewed a student who wanted to take a course and the reason she gave was this: "You just know when something is meant for you, when it's right." When that happens to you, you start looking things up, asking questions and following leads that will bring you a greater familiarity with the subject. For example, when I wanted to visit Savannah, I went through one guide book after another, studied maps and asked numerous people who had visited the city where I should stay and what I should do. This was not like a business trip that might take me there by accident, but a location I had always wanted to visit. Thus, I was actively learning everything I could to maximize my experience.

Developing the third level of awareness as a habit of

mindfulness also works to bring a passive mind into better service to you. A friend of mine told me about a time when he was going through a relationship crisis and one day, in the midst of his pain and turmoil, he got very quiet. Not numb, not angry, just quiet. He felt that he was allowing his life to be decided by someone else, so he allowed the stillness to nest in him for a few hours. He wasn't thinking anything in particular or obsessing over the relationship, but just being quiet. As the day wore on, he began to emerge from the passive stillness into a feeling that he should act, and all at once it became clear what he needed to do to take charge of his life. He called the other person, told her what he needed to say and moved on. In this case, he allowed the mind/body relationship to process itself until it yielded a form of awareness that motivated him to engage with the situation actively rather than passively. He trusted it and it produced.

At the second level of awareness, although we are more focused, we typically forget most of what we were focused on. The third level makes it more a part of us, like breathing in the odor of someone you love and always knowing that smell, whether or not the person is present.

In other words, awareness is on a continuum, and the third level *involves* you. You feel what you are focusing on flow into yourself, and you retain knowledge of it for a longer time and in a more profound way. It's more like learning something that will make a difference in your life as compared to learning items for an exam. And the learning, while engaged and alert, is also more relaxed and satisfying.

You have a lot of mental energy, but all too often it's easier to allow it to weaken through a lazy mind. The more you practice focusing, the more available your mental energy will be and the better it will serve you. It requires discipline and the desire to achieve this state, but it can become a habit. The better you get at it, the more likely it is that you will be receptive to your intuition and to achieving the state described in the following chapter—the peak moment of flow that can affirm your bliss.

Exercises

1. Find an activity that you do routinely. The next time you do it, select something within that activity you can focus on, and notice the difference between your level of awareness when it's just routine and your level of awareness when you're paying more attention. Write a one-page essay about the way these two states of mind feel and what the experience showed you. Then talk about how the difference may help you to find your bliss.

2. Select a subject that you've been wanting to learn more about and do some research, noting how it feels to learn in a manner that is engaged and enjoyable. Write a one-page essay about how it feels and how you might apply this same experience to understanding your life direction.

★

You are steps away from putting this all together: Finding your bliss using intuition, concentration, awareness of your feelings, discovery of your blind spots and the development of your abilities. It's time to see what goes into that heightened experience that signals when bliss is at hand.

thirteen

Recognizing Bliss

★

American psychologist Abraham Maslow reached a point in his career where he decided that psychologists were putting too much effort into the diagnosis of disease and not enough into health. People enjoy life and are motivated to achieve, find and fulfill their potential. With that in mind, he tried to form an idea of what human perfection might be like. What was the model, or ideal, of health and well-being? Who showed us what self-improvement and ecstasy really could be?

Our motivations in life can be viewed through a hierarchy of needs, from the most primitive survival needs to the highest levels of joy. The lowest needs must be met first, such as satisfying hunger and the need for shelter; then we seek love and self-esteem; moving on up, we strive toward becoming self-actualized. At this level, we may move toward what Maslow called a peak experience.

Peak experiences are characterized by feelings of bliss, spontaneity, crystallized focus, heightened ability and energy, an awareness of the richness of the moment, freedom from anxiety and a sense of merging in harmony with environment. Maslow studied people who had these experiences and discovered that after they had peak moments, they approached the activity that produced these feelings with great joy and anticipation. They felt they could transcend their ordinary limits and move beyond mundane routine, while also strengthening their sense of personal identity. They felt more fully themselves and more attuned with the joy of being alive. Maslow believed that the great mystics of any given religion were probably people who experienced these peak moments—as if they were united with some supreme being.

Such ecstasy, however, was not to be sought for its own sake, cutting it loose from one's achievements and from one's attachment to others. Maslow thought that pursuing self-actualization as a totally selfish goal only contributes to narcissism and, thus, a loss of compassion. It also cannot be pursued as a pure state. Just as a figure needs a background to stand out, so a peak experience needs ordinary experiences to be fully appreciated. It must have a context.

Maslow listed sixteen qualities of a peak experience:

1. You feel whole and unified.

2. You feel more yourself even while you merge into your activity.

3. You feel that you utilize your capacities to the fullest.

4. Your activity feels effortless and easy, even though you are working at your greatest capacity.

5. You feel that you are the prime mover, the initiator.

6. You feel free from blocks and hindrances, like fear and self-criticism.

7. Your activity is spontaneous and responsive.

8. You feel that you are interacting with others and your environment in a harmonious manner.

9. You recognize your uniqueness and individuality.

10. You feel "all there" and attuned to your surroundings.

11. You feel as if you are pure psyche or spirit.

12. You feel complete and fully present in the moment.

13. Your expressions in the moment tend toward poetry and rhapsody.

14. You have a sense of closure or climax in what you're doing.

15. Playfulness is part of the experience.

16. You feel lucky or blessed.

When the Inner Self moves us forward and we're in touch with that activity that most closely expresses our gifts, we have these experiences. We find physical and mental resources that may even surprise us. We discover and feel wonderful about our unique capacities, as if we have tapped into the essence of life itself. We are in touch with our self-affirming center. Now we need to learn how to sustain these moments.

Exercise

Return to chapter three and look over the ideas about flow. Read what you wrote in your notebook about your own experiences. If you have anything to add on the notion of self-actualization and peak moments, add it now.

★ BLISS AND THE ART OF HEIGHTENED EXPERIENCE ★

Peak moments are essential to the concept of bliss. They become markers that help us know we're on the right track. You might achieve some success in your career through effort and brains, but that would not necessarily affirm that you have found your bliss. If there are no moments of joy or the feeling that you are actualizing your potential, then it's likely you are only achieving success in the material sense but not actually transcending toward bliss. In that state, you seek the feeling of a larger self, a sense of growing and dynamism.

Peak moments arise out the deepening of flow. You move from energy and excitement into periods of supreme ability or enjoyment, and you can make them occur more often. People generally view those unexpected moments of flow as being unique pockets of energy with a beginning and an end, which can be depleted and might never return. However, the feeling of flow, or the peak moment, which affirms that we're on the proper track, is less spontaneous than we might believe. It is the result of focus and concentration, which in themselves require good health, rest and a clarity of purpose. The stages of concentration involve the art of stillness and an awareness of what we need to arrange in our lives to maximize the deepening process.

★ A Word About Commitment ★

To build a life structure, you need to be committed to it. While I will show you some ways to enhance the conditions that bring about flow and to help you achieve more frequent peak moments, it's also important to maintain your vision during "down time."

When you know what you want to do, you still need a plan. Peak moments won't carry you completely. You need to make a commitment to finding some way to feed your vision. There are five principles in this type of commitment:

1. Keep your vision as the central reason for why you pursue certain activities, such as skills training or networking. Make your pursuits values-driven, with a long-term perspective.

2. Draw on your proven strengths. Use what has worked for you to maintain your confidence level.

3. Recognize your limits.

4. Be adaptable. If what you want to do doesn't work out in quite the way you envisioned, you may need to fine-tune your vision to fit your circumstances. Bliss is not about living in dreams, but about working within reality to find your unique life plan.

5. Be resolved. When you know what you want, you need to keep affirming your goals and do what's necessary to get your skills and connections up to snuff.

Commitment is about persistence, patience and clear intentions. It requires faith, hope and trust. Your own integrity depends on maintaining the continuity of your vision. You are living your values in a way that should enhance your life. As Thoreau said, "A man must find his occasions in himself. . . . If one advances confidently in the direction of his dreams, and endeavors to live the life which he has imagined, he will meet with a success unexpected in common hours." To find and follow your bliss, you must remain committed to it despite the obstacles.

Exercise

Check what you believe is your bliss against the five principles above and adjust your plan accordingly. Write down how you will commit yourself to your pursuit.

★ The Energy of the Quiet Mind ★

In many of the exercises listed in previous chapters, such as those in chapters eight and nine, you were asked to quiet your mind. Too often we view that as bringing ourselves into a state just short of falling asleep. However, maintaining flow via a still mind is about tapping into the energy made available by ridding ourselves of mental distractions. You actually intensify your mental state. Before you look at the steps listed below, take some time to ponder the value of the quieted mind.

We marvel at the intense degree of concentration sustained by athletes and artists. That they can sustain it for so long seems beyond the abilities of most of us. They amaze us with their unusual stamina and extraordinary performances. However, all of us are capable of peak performance, of quality and of creativity in what we do.

The focused, receptive mind is relaxed and alert. That means you need to be well-nourished and rested, as well as have a regular exercise routine. These amazing abilities are only available to people who take the time and acquire the discipline to keep themselves mentally and physically in shape.

Becoming still progresses through two stages: (1) physically relaxing, and (2) allowing your mind to grow more patient and attentive. You are ready without being tense.

There is power in the deeply hidden self, a wealth of spontaneous creativity to be tapped. It is the avenue toward mental clarity. While we sometimes associate this state with loneliness and vulnerability, it is really about self-strengthening solitude.

Honing your ability to be still yet alert will see you through the periods of confusion that often accompany movement in a new direction (which may be important if your bliss requires dramatic change and the acquisition of new skills). A quiet mind clears away the background noise. It translates energy from tension into mental stimulation.

★ CONDITIONS FOR FLOW ENHANCEMENT ★

As I've stated before, flow occurs when you know what you are doing and love it so much that you become part of it. Flow is a natural result of working within your bliss. It seems to move through stages, from preparation to onset to a deep, trancelike state and then back to the ordinary world. The result is a feeling of accomplishment and perhaps even surprise at how much you accomplished or how well you did it.

At the stage of onset, there is a heightened feeling of energy, excitement and active engagement with the work you are doing. The pace increases, and an easy rhythm develops. "I'll just start drawing like mad," said an artist. Even while concentration deepens and becomes more focused, the work is fluid. The field of perception narrows, and manual dexterity increases.

During the deepest stage, you transcend all mechanics and operate in such a way that you feel like you're on automatic pilot. Actions are unmediated by conscious processes. There is an integrated, single-minded attention to the project at hand. "At this stage," said an editor who loves his work, "the writing itself becomes the reality." The physical realities of your environment recede, and confidence and control move the experience forward. Only when the goal is achieved—unless there is some major interruption—do you come out of this deep concentration.

The foundation for flow includes a positive attitude, a good self-image and physical well-being. You'll need to establish clear goals, have a good match between your skills and your activity, have a sense of opportunity and practice flow-enhancing habits.

Controlling those moments of peak experience so you can make them occur on a regular basis is not the same as forcing them to happen. It's about calling on your skill of inner direction, coupled with discipline and flow-friendly conditions. The desire for flow should not become obsessive. What you want to experience is joy and confidence, not desperation or tension. Positive feelings are the result of getting into flow and, like the water you carried in a bucket, should not become the focus.

Your level of performance is directly related to your self-image. How you feel about yourself will influence how you view your pursuits. I once worked on a project that had an idealistic motive—helping people better themselves. That sounded good to me, but once I got involved, I came up against a haphazard bureaucratic administration that put constant hurdles in my way. No matter how much I wanted to be involved in the project itself, I found it impossible to avoid the stress and annoyance that came from the management. The worse the working conditions got, the worse I felt about myself and the less joy I took in whatever results I achieved, which translated into having less enthusiasm around the people I was trying to help. Finally, I resigned. I knew enough to realize that if I felt angry and stressed with those who ran the program, it would continue to spill over into my work. That's not bliss.

This same kind of transference works in any endeavor. If you don't feel good about who you are, you will not feel good about what you are doing. Conversely, if you are relatively free of self-doubt, it is more likely that you will experience pleasurable absorption.

Flow most often occurs when you are challenged by an activity but not intimidated by it because you know you possess the skills to meet the challenge. Setting your sights too low fails to engage your concentration to the degree necessary for flow to occur. On the other hand, setting them too high can result in frustration and anxiety. You need to have the ability to fully concentrate on what needs to be done to meet the challenges, which means developing self-motivation skills, perseverance and commitment.

Visualization exercises can help in that regard, so you can actually see yourself doing the activity. Mental agility is also helpful, in case you need to think of alternative ways of doing something or you need to reframe an event or goal. See whatever you are doing as part of a larger process and keep envisioning how it all fits together with what you ultimately want to do.

According to the research, in order to achieve flow, you need to have clear goals, such as a project that needs to be finished. You also need opportunities to get into the conditions under which flow can occur. The more opportunities you can find for flow-productive activities, the more skilled you become at recognizing those conditions that affect it. I recall speaking to an author about his rather sporadic experiences of flow. He wanted them to happen more often because during these times, his work was so much better and more enjoyable. However, he was frustrated about how to make that happen. I asked him the following questions:

"When has the experience of flow happened most often?"

"When things are quiet and uninterrupted."

"Do you answer your own phone?"

"Yes."

"How often does it ring?"

"Pretty often. About every twenty minutes or so."

"I see. And is your work area in a private place?"

"No. I often have to watch the kids."

I didn't need to ask more. Although this man engaged in flow-enhancing work, he corrupted his own opportunities with constant distractions. He knew which conditions would work best, but he failed to utilize them.

You need to establish habits or rituals that work for you. If you work best in a quiet setting or at a certain time of day, use that to your advantage. If you prefer having music, put it on as often as possible. If you work best with a clear and tidy work space, then eliminate the clutter.

Before you begin on a project in which you hope to experience flow, be sure everything you need is ready and your tools or machines are in working condition. A clergyman told me that before he starts to write a sermon, which invariably puts him in flow, he makes sure that he has spoken to everyone he needs to and has gathered together all of the texts he will need. Nothing stops flow like the inability to find something you need *right now* or an instrument that does not work correctly. Be prepared.

Some people also think that mental rehearsal is an important part of preparation. They visually put themselves through the motions before embarking on a complicated project. Once they actually start to work, it seems much easier because they have already "seen" all the steps.

One person told me that she must have a sense of peace in her relationships before she can move into flow; otherwise, she'll be thinking about the relationships rather than her work. If you need to get your emotional life in order to feel prepared, do so.

You can tell from your own rhythms and experiences what is most likely to work for you. It's up to you to make them work.

Exercise

Pick three separate times when you have experienced flow. For each, describe the conditions, both physical and mental. What patterns do you see? Compare them to any other experience of flow that you can recall. Based on the discussion above, what would you need to set up the right conditions for you to experience flow again? Write down your thoughts.

Keep track of other flow experiences as you have them.

★ RECOGNIZING BLISS—THE AUTHENTIC MOMENT ★

The whole concept of bliss—that you have an interior design for your best life pursuit—is connected to the notion of authenticity, which implies being your own unique self. The notion of the authentic life has a long history. Socrates insisted that the morally unexamined life is not worth living and Aristotle sought to define the contented soul as the person who has balance. Other thinkers have made authentic existence their cornerstone: Be who you are. Be mindful. Be engaged.

So what does that really mean? How does it translate into ordinary lives? Authenticity is self-actualization, with an emphasis on integrity. When we find our authentic selves, we find our bliss. We are choosing to follow the path that is most right for us.

I've always been inspired by what the nineteenth-century German philosopher, Friedrich Nietzsche, said about how to live. He urged us to make from our lives a work of art. That is, we should embrace our fate and live as creatively as we possibly can. More books are being published that promote this message, but they make it sound as if it's just a matter of becoming aware or of being sincere. It's much more than that. We can establish a core self through which our lives can actually be made into a work of art—an original, signed by us. But we have to work at it. "No one is coming" to give it to us.

"How do you measure a year in a life?" A single year contains 525,600 minutes—at least according to a song in the Broadway musical, Rent. That's a lot of minutes, but making each one count is really the point. I know one person who heard that song and, shaken, she left a failed marriage and mundane job to start living her life. "I measured a year in my life by trips to the mall and endless television shows," she opined. "I could not believe how much time I had wasted." Now she manages her own business and does a lot of volunteer work.

How do others define an authentic life? Some people think it means getting something made by a designer, others view it as an outgrowth of something in the soul. "I am only authentically myself when I constantly examine who I am," said a social worker, "not in contrast to those around me, but comparing what I'm thinking to what I do. My life will be real, and not a lie, when I consistently translate my feelings into pure living—and when what I do matches what I feel."

Demographer Paul Ray, who lives in San Francisco and is vice president of the market research firm, American Lives, Inc., believes that the search for the authentic life is a growing phenomenon. Those who seek what's real, according to his surveys, turn away from fashion and status. They tend to be conscious of the environment, to hate waste and to seek spiritual substance in their lives.

★ AUTHENTICITY AND BLISS ★

We find our destinies by recovering what has been lost of our intrinsic selves and following the pattern that emerges. Only then can we experience harmony with life itself. Our authentic inner self becomes a sort of "prime mover." It senses our direction and urges us toward it. When we're in harmony, we feel a sense of security and inner peace. If we deny who we are or fail to follow our path, we may feel sick, unhappy or stressed.

In terms of bliss, the need for authenticity influenced MaryLynn, a marketing director, to listen to her inner voice. She then created a way for people to meet regularly to discuss issues that would help to improve their lives. In 1991, she started the Salon des Philosophes in her hometown, inviting speakers to address the pressing concerns of mindful living. She changed venues in 1995 to bring these interactive discussions to cyberspace with the Electronic Salon.

"I took what was uniquely my talent," she says, "and used it the best way I could. Living authentically is not a selfish thing. You can use your talent to give to the world. In the process of reaching into myself and finding my need to connect with other people, I was able to create something that others enjoyed. The Electronic Salon was a big success, despite the fact that when I first proposed it, it was met with great skepticism. To live authentically, you have to have the courage to follow what your imagination and intuition are telling you. The only thing that makes life genuine is what is inside you. You have to write your own play and star in it!"

This is similar to what Pelli Wheaton, a therapist in Stockton, New Jersey, believes. She introduces herself to new clients as a counselor who means business. Less than 10 percent of the American people, she says, are on the road that leads to becoming their own true selves. In that case, few people are out there finding their bliss. It takes courage and discipline to break patterns that trap us in the ideas that others have for us.

"During the first half of life," she says, "we're just trying to survive. It's during the second part that we get the opportunity to begin to feel truly alive." The significant factor is the way we notice the passing of time. By this, she can tell the difference between those who live authentically and those who do not: "I look for a joy of life, a radiance. Awareness has to be used constructively. We have to notice what nature tells us—that death is a fact of life. All of life involves the passing of time, and how we use it is the measure of our humanity. We have to value our time and use it well."

If people become frightened by the way time is passing, she points out, they may seek to control it or find ways to pretend that this fact is not real. Society often rewards this kind of behavior by promoting youth. Yet the authentic life is based on truth: "The truth is that we age, so the best we can do is recognize our power to decide how we will use our time. Putting it to good use will yield an abundance."

So how do we measure a year in a life? Each person, it seems, must decide what his or her own soul's code instructs. A clear vision, an inner voice, an appreciation of the right convergence of life events and choosing real over imitation are important factors in living authentically and finding bliss.

Exercise

Write an essay about what the authentic life means to you, especially in terms of the examined life. Then include a paragraph about how you believe what you just wrote is related to finding your bliss. Write something about the idea that finding your bliss implies that you are spending your time well.

Whatever your bliss turns out to be, pursuing it will energize and empower you. You'll feel the strong responses to it described as joy, inner peace, purpose and creativity. You'll feel fully alive and your best moments will involve the perception that you have merged with what you want to do. Doors will open and connections will be made that seem like an act of grace. "This is it!" you'll say. "This is right for me."

★ BLISS REVIEW ★

I have mentioned that there are certain signs for when you are, or are not, following your bliss. Typically, you will feel them in your body, so the more aware you are of your physical state, the more likely it is that you will be able to discern your best direction. Let me review them with you:

Signs that you *are not* on your path:

* stress
* depression
* depletion

* inertia
* chronic anger
* chronic anxiety
* illness
* fear
* feeling of constant pressure
* the need to control what is happening
* constant external blocks to your goals
* feeling that you are always struggling
* numerous good friends who question that this
  activity is right for you
* the lack of joy in your accomplishments
* dullness; not looking forward to anything
* dread or despair
* feeling that life is a curse

Signs that you *are* on your path:
* moments of ecstasy and euphoria
* sense of direction and purpose
* ease of standing up under pressure
* health in mind and body
* sense of inner peace
* feeling that you are fully using your gifts
* mental clarity, clear vision
* evidence of creativity—that you are living your life as
  a work of art
* excellence in your work
* momentum
* taking initiative and using self-discipline
* excitement about your future
* feeling of challenge without being overwhelmed
* freedom from negative stress, such as depression
* able to connect with others from within the pursuit
* an active dream life that affirms it
* feeling alive

* sense of connection to a larger self or force; feeling of expansion
* sense of grace
* conviction
* early hints in your childhood about the direction you should take
* open doors along the way; overcoming obstacles via synchronistic interventions
* feelings of mind/body integration
* relaxed alertness
* enlightenment, enhancement, self-creation

Exercise

If you know your bliss, compare it to those signs listed above and write about how closely it matches. If you only have an idea of what you think it might be, write about how your future potential pursuit matches the list.

Keep in mind that bliss is a process that involves several layers. Although it is moved by spiritual forces, it is not magic. You need to do some work to become self-aware and to be proactive. Bliss is the closest we can come to living our lives as a work of art. When we are doing what we are meant to do, we will do it well. In that way, we offer the world the best that we have and thereby make it a better place to live, for ourselves and for others.

Epilogue

★

"Life shrinks or expands," said Anais Nin, "in proportion to one's courage."

If I were to conjure up an image for active imagination as a way to summarize these ideas, I would bring up my former mentor, Richard Wood. He was a philosophy professor in Arizona who insisted on developing a sense of personal accountability in what we say and think. Nothing was more important to him than truth. If I were to create a safe space for myself, honesty would be the foundation.

So I would bring him forth in my imagination in his cowboy boots and shiny belt buckle, his short dark hair and mustache, pacing back and forth across the front of a classroom and peering at us with the most intense gaze, looking for the person with whom to set an example. If you had something to fear, he could be intimidating, but if you were open to learning, you could gain some powerful wisdom from him. Through him, I can easily think about the elements that go into the way we each must uniquely live our lives.

Following your bliss requires self-awareness, mental flexibility, mental agility and vision. That vision must be substantial, having a spiritual quality so that you can ask, "Is this what makes my life worth living?" That question is a measuring point that would make Wood nod in approval. It gives you a means to find your center.

You need to be able use any tool that would help you figure out your values, your skills and your ability to hone a sense of direction. That means you must be able to move through the stages of awareness into deep concentration—into flow. It is the optimum moment of following your bliss, a sign that you are on the right track. Flow feels to me as I felt in Wood's classroom—alert, prepared and ready to move with the energy present to do my best work.

I'm well aware that Dick Wood followed his bliss in the classroom. He could teach a three-hour class and keep going. He got into flow, there is no doubt in my mind. From him I learned that teaching is an art—and for me, that translates into the idea that whatever your bliss turns out to be, it should make your life a work of art.

When you're moving toward your bliss, you'll realize it doesn't matter if "no one is coming," because you'll be delighted to be there. You'll be at home.

Belitz, Charlene and Meg Lundstrom. *The Power of Flow.* New York: Three Rivers Press, 1998.

Bennett, Hal Zina and Susan J. Sparrow. *Follow Your Bliss.* New York: Avon, 1988.

Blevins, William L. *Your Family, Your Self: How to Analyze Your Family System to Understand Yourself and Achieve More Satisfying Relationships With Your Loved Ones.* Oakland, CA: New Harbinger Publications, 1993.

Buchalter, Gail. "A Power Will Guide You—If You Let It." *Parade Magazine,* April 4, 1999.

Carson, Ben and Gregg A. Lewis. *The Big Picture.* New York: Zondervan, 1999.

Cohen, Alan. *Joy Is My Compass: Taking the Risk to Follow Your Bliss.* Carslbad, CA: HayHouse, Inc., 1996.

Colt, George Howe. "The Power of Dreams." *Life,* September, 1995.

Colt, Lee. *Listening: How to Increase Awareness of Your Inner Guide.* Carlsbad, CA: Hay House Inc., 1996.

Combs, Allan and Mark Holland. *Synchronicity: Science, Myth, and the Trickster.* New York: Paragon House, 1990.

Csikszentmihalyi, Mihaly. *Flow: The Psychology of Optimal Experience.* New York: Harper & Row, 1989.

de Saint-Exupery, Antoine. *The Little Prince.* New York: Harcourt Brace Jovanovich, 1956.

Dillard, Annie. *Pilgrim at Tinker Creek.* New York: Harper Collins Publishers, 1998.

Garfield, Charles. *Peak Performers: The New Heroes of American Business.* New York: Avon, 1986.

Gendlin, Eugene. *Focusing.* New York: Bantam, 1979.

Gross, Ronald. *Peak Learning.* Los Angeles: Jeremy P. Tarcher, Inc., 1991.

Herrigel, Eugen. *Zen in the Art of Archery.* New York: Random House, 1999.

Hickam, Homer. *October Sky* (previously *Rocket Boys*). New York: Bantam, 1999.

Hillman, James. *The Soul's Code: In Search of Character and Calling*. New York: Warner, 1997.

Jung, Carl G. *The Archetypes and the Collective Unconscious*. Edited by Michael Fordham. Translated by R.F. Hull. Princeton, NJ: Princeton University Press, 1980.

———. *The Basic Writings of C.G. Jung*. Edited by Violet De Laszlo. New York: Modern Library, 1993.

Kierkegaard, Soren. *Concluding Unscientific Postscript to Philosophical Fragments*. Translated by David F. Swenson and Walter Lowrie. Princeton, NJ: Princeton University Press [1846], 1968.

———. *The Sickness Unto Death: A Christian Psychological Exposition for Upbuilding and Awakening*. Translated by H.V. Hong and E.H. Hong. Princeton, NJ: Princeton University Press, 1980.

Lamott, Anne. *Bird by Bird: Some Instructions on Writing and Life*. New York: Anchor, 1994.

———. *Traveling Mercies: Some Thoughts on Faith*. New York: Pantheon, 1999.

Langer, Ellen. *Mindfulness*. New York: Addison Wesley Longman, Inc., 1989.

Miller, William. *Make Friends With Your Shadow*. Minneapolis, MN: Augsburg Publishing, 1981.

Orlick, Terry. *In Pursuit of Excellence*, 2nd ed. Champaign, IL: Leisure Press, 1990.

Pert, Candace. *Molecules of Emotion: Why You Feel the Way You Feel*. New York: Scribner, 1997.

Plato. *The Collected Dialogues of Plato, Including the Letters*. Edited by Edith Hamilton and Huntington Cairns. Princeton, NJ: Princeton University Press, 1961.

Ramsland, Katherine. *The Art of Learning*. Albany, NY: State University of New York Press, 1992.

———. *Dean Koontz: A Writer's Biography*. New York: Harper Collins, 1997.

———. "The Best of All Possible Worlds: Is It Already Within Us?" *Magical Blend*, October 1992.

———. *Prism of the Night: A Biography of Anne Rice*. New York: Dutton, 1991.

Shapiro, Robin. *Riding the Wind: Healing the Whole Person*. Sunstar Publishing, Ltd., 1997.

Smith, Scott. *A Simple Plan*. New York: St. Martin's Press, 1994.

Spretnak, Charlene. *The Resurgence of the Real*. New York: Routledge, 1999.

Styron, William. *Darkness Visible: A Memoir of Madness*. New York: Vintage, 1992.

———. *Sophie's Choice*. New York: Vintage, 1992.

Suzuki, D.T. *Zen and Japanese Culture*. Princeton, NJ: Princeton University Press, 1972.

Vaughan, Alan. *Incredible Coincidence: The Baffling World of Synchronicity*. New York: Ballantine, 1979.

Wilson, Colin. *The Essential Colin Wilson*. Berkeley, CA: Celestial Arts, 1986.

Wolinksy, Stephen. *Trances People Live*. Fall Village, CT: The Bramble Company, 1991.

Zilbergeld, Bernie and Arnold Lazarus. *Mind Power: Getting What You Want Through Mental Training*. Boston: Little Brown, 1987.

WATCH FOR THESE OTHER TITLES FROM WALKING STICK PRESS

A Year in the Life—Using a masterful blend of guidance, weekly idea prompts and self-evaluation advice, author and poet Sheila Bender nurtures you through one full year of soul searching through journal writing.
#10656/$14.99/224 pages/paperback

Things That Tick Me Off (A Guided Journal)—Without a doubt, everyone has their own list of things that can really make them angry. This guide helps you vent your frustrations and alleviate stress as you explore emotional causes and effects to develop a greater sense of peace and balance.
#10701/$14.99/144 pages/hardcover

The Book of Self-Acquaintance (A Guided Journal)—This guide encourages you to employ various methods of descriptive writing to reflect on your life and learn from the past. Open-ended prompts serve as intriguing starting points, enabling you to examine who you are and what you really value.
#10704/$14.99/144 pages/hardcover

From Dreams to Discovery (A Guided Journal)—Using a unique mix of instruction and prompts, licensed psychotherapist Joan Mazza guides you through the dreamwork process, showing how to interpret dream symbols, characters and the messages they're sending.
#10692/$14.99/144 pages/hardcover

What Really Matters to Me (A Guided Journal)—Inspired by stories and prompts, you'll learn to shed the stresses and tribulations that burden you and focus on what's most important in your life. Through these realizations, you'll discover the knowledge and awareness that will help you maintain your inner peace.
#10688/$14.99/144 pages/hardcover

From Me to You—This is the perfect guide for anyone who wants to write sincere personal letters, but struggles with expressing how they really feel. A combination of friendly instruction and model letters shows you how to create cherished letters of love, gratitude, sympathy, forgiveness, apology and comfort.
#10706/$14.99/192 pages/paperback